"Reading *The Ministry We Need* was precisely the encouragement I needed! I have never read a book for pastors more thoroughly biblical, emphatically practical, and relentlessly challenging. Though unafraid to grapple with the most difficult questions of ministry, the warm devotional tone of the Rogers engaged my heart as well as my head."

—Hershael W. York,
The Southern Baptist Theological Seminary

"Pastors Jeremy, Jordan, and Tony Rogers know that pastoral ministry can be tough. They have been sustained by their conviction that the Scriptures are sufficient to guide them through all the difficulties of ministry. . . . If you are a pastor, *The Ministry We Need* is a book you need."

—Matt Queen,
Southwestern Baptist Theological Seminary

"You will not read a more encouraging book this year than *The Ministry We Need*. Three pastors unpack Paul's address to the Ephesian elders in Acts 20 in a masterful fashion. Here is analysis and diagnosis to be sure, but as the authors tell us, 'remedy is paramount.' This book is indeed tonic for the new pastor, the experienced pastor, or the discouraged pastor. Let the Rogers trio open up Paul's own heart for ministry to speak to you and your ministry. Highly recommended!"

—David L. Allen,
Southwestern Baptist Theological Seminary

"These pages come from a remarkable family of effective ministers. Using Scripture and personal experience and gathering illustrations from dozens of ministers in our ministerial world, Tony, Jeremy, and Jordan have penned a remarkable book. Read it and be blessed. Practice it and successfully navigate the complicated ministerial landscape of our contemporary world."

—Jimmy Draper,
president emeritus, LifeWay

"Tony Rogers and his two sons, Jordan and Jeremy, provide an inspirational and instructional guidebook for ministry. They use personal antidotes and significant quotes from well-known and unknown servants of the Lord. Included are warnings about the pitfalls in ministry. This well-researched and Scripture-filled book is a must-read for those entering the ministry and those continuing to serve. Read it and reread it!"

—JAMES W. RICHARDS,
executive director emeritus, Southern Baptists of Texas Convention

"Not one chapter fails to provide a wealth of reproof, encouragement, and correction for one serving the Lord in pastoral ministry. The honest, insightful, and challenging instruction is a feast for the souls of God's under-shepherds. *The Ministry We Need* is a must-read for those serving in ministry as well as for those preparing for the ministry, and is one that should be read annually throughout one's ministry."

—BEN AWBREY,
Midwestern Baptist Theological Seminary

"*The Ministry We Need* is a timely reminder to pastors that standing on the foundation of God's word has never been more imperative. We currently live in a world where relevance reigns over truth. Jeremy, Jordan, and Tony do a fantastic job emphasizing the need for pastoral humility, ministry boldness, and sacrificial service. This read will invigorate you to seek your area of leadership with more intentionality and authenticity. I cannot recommend this read enough!"

—SHANE PRUITT,
author of *9 Common Lies Christians Believe*

The Ministry We Need

The Ministry We Need

Paul's Ancient Farewell—
The Pastor's Present Calling (Acts 20:17–38)

Jeremy A. Rogers
Jordan N. Rogers
Tony A. Rogers

Foreword by Michael Card

RESOURCE *Publications* · Eugene, Oregon

THE MINISTRY WE NEED
Paul's Ancient Farewell—The Pastor's Present Calling (Acts 20:17–38)

Copyright © 2022 Jeremy A. Rogers, Jordan N. Rogers, and Tony A. Rogers. All rights reserved. Except for brief quotations in critical publications or reviews, no part of this book may be reproduced in any manner without prior written permission from the publisher. Write: Permissions, Wipf and Stock Publishers, 199 W. 8th Ave., Suite 3, Eugene, OR 97401.

Resource Publications
An Imprint of Wipf and Stock Publishers
199 W. 8th Ave., Suite 3
Eugene, OR 97401

www.wipfandstock.com

PAPERBACK ISBN: 978-1-6667-1288-9
HARDCOVER ISBN: 978-1-6667-1289-6
EBOOK ISBN: 978-1-6667-1290-2

MAY 12, 2022 11:29 AM

Unless otherwise noted, Scripture quotations are from the ESV® Bible (The Holy Bible, English Standard Version®), Copyright © 2001 by Crossway, a publishing ministry of Good News Publishers. Used by permission. All rights reserved.

Dedicated to all those who have taught us to preach and pastor in church, class, seminar, dissertation, or life. More importantly, they taught us about *the ministry we need*.

Iron sharpens iron, and one person sharpens another
— Proverbs 27:17 —

Dr. David Allen, Dr. Denny Autrey, Dr. Ben Awbrey,
Dr. Russ Barksdale, Dr. John Bisagno, Dr. James Bryant,
Dr. Lamar Cooper, Dr. Bill Curtis, Dr. George B. Davis Sr.,
Dr. Lanny Elmore, Dr. H. Leroy Metts, Dr. Dwayne Milioni,
Dr. Bob Overton, Dr. Kenneth Parker, Dr. Jim Richards,
Dr. Jim Shaddix, Dr. Don L. Stephens,
Dr. Alan Streett, Dr. Chuck Ward,
Dr. C. Richard Wells, Dr. Hershael York

What you have heard from me in the presence of many witnesses, commit to faithful men who will be able to teach others also
— 2 Timothy 2:2 —

> "The minister's singular focus is to consistently show how the kingdom of God, and King Jesus, affect everything about the lives of his listeners."
> —*A CONSISTENT MINISTRY*

> "A daily, intentional, and genuine magnification of God will subsequently lead to the destruction of pride in our hearts."
> —*A HUMBLE MINISTRY*

> "There are certainly many wonderful and glorious aspects to the gospel ministry, however, we must be prepared for the necessary vulnerability as well as the certain difficulty and opposition we will encounter."
> —*A READY MINISTRY*

> "To be bold in ministry, you must be hopeful of God's faithfulness to fulfill His promises."
> —*A BOLD MINISTRY*

> "If our interest is *gospel-centered* preaching, we might ask ourselves, "What is missing from our sermons?" Good thought, but the better, more insightful question might be – "*Who* is missing from our sermons?""
> —*A GOSPEL-CENTERED MINISTRY*

> "Lack of personal holiness, especially concerning moral purity is a deplorable thing for the man of God."
> —*A SPIRIT-LED MINISTRY*

"Preach preacher, God's listening!" and calling His ministers to complete the mission they have been given for His glory.
—A MISSION-MINDED MINISTRY

"When our tongues fail us, God's Word reminds us that it is our heart that failed us first."
—A BLAMELESS AND COMPLETE MINISTRY

'The calamity of a pastor's fall will always affect the people he has been shepherding."
—A VIGILANT MINISTRY

"No man God calls to His ministry is expected to be the source of his own strength or the cause of enduring preservation."
—A DEPENDENT MINISTRY

"When the minister begins to look at the people of God – the church, as a cow to milk instead of sheep to feed, then he is a hireling and forfeits his privilege to minister in God's name."
—A CONTENT AND HARDWORKING MINISTRY

"The more we pray for people by name, the more our affections for them are stirred."
—A RELATIONAL MINISTRY

Table of Contents

Foreword by Michael Card | xi

Preface | xiii

Acknowledgments | xvii

Abbreviations | xviii

Chapter 1	A Consistent Ministry | 1 (Acts 20:17–18)
Chapter 2	A Humble Ministry | 9 (Acts 20:19a)
Chapter 3	A Ready Ministry | 16 (Acts 20:19b)
Chapter 4	A Bold Ministry | 25 (Acts 20:20)
Chapter 5	A Gospel-centered Ministry | 32 (Acts 20:21)
Chapter 6	A Spirit-led Ministry | 43 (Acts 20:22–23)
Chapter 7	A Mission-minded Ministry | 57 (Acts 20:24)
Chapter 8	A Blameless and Complete Ministry | 66 (Acts 20:25–27)

Chapter 9	A Vigilant Ministry | 83
	(Acts 20:28–31)
Chapter 10	A Dependent Ministry | 92
	(Acts 20:32)
Chapter 11	A Content and Hardworking Ministry | 98
	(Acts 20:33–35)
Chapter 12	A Relational Ministry | 114
	(Acts 20:36–38)
Conclusion	Put Your Hand to the Plow | 121

Bibliography | 129

Foreword

PAUL IS A PARADIGM. A paradigm Pharisee, a paradigm persecutor, and a paradigm apostle. He is an exemplary pastor and church planter. His life provides a perfect archetype of the radical reversal that Jesus refers to as being "born again." The Paul of Acts chapter 8 is simply not the same person as the Paul of Acts chapter 9.

By the time we see him in chapter 20, he has traveled over most of the Roman world, principally with his close companion Barnabas. He has suffered and preached his heart out, been mistaken for a god, and endured imprisonment. In Athens he impressed the wise men of the Areopagus with his radical message of resurrection. Sometime after planting a church in Corinth with his new partner, Timothy, he ends up in Ephesus. For three years he poured himself into training disciples and performing miracles of healing. Eventually a conflict between the silversmiths (who sold idols of Artemis), and Paul led to a major riot, and he chose to leave the city.

Setting out once more, he left for Macedonia, by way of Troas and eventually stopping in Miletus. From there Paul sent a message to the elders of the Ephesian church, some thirty miles away, asking them to come. Knowing their life situation as he does, Paul understood they needed encouragement. More importantly, he knows this will be his last chance to pour himself into their lives. So, it is a farewell speech, a final testament, containing all of the encouragement and advice he would leave to the leaders of that ancient church; that he would leave to the leaders of our churches today.

It was an emotional time. There were tears and embracing, as they tried to cope with his mentioning that he would never see them again. Through his tears he spoke of "savage wolves," they must be on guard against. He was equipping them, and us, with the direction and encouragement they, and we, so badly need. They must remain alert and follow the example he set for them over the three years he lived among them. It is the only address given to followers of Christ that Luke, who was almost certainly an eyewitness, provides. The final words of advice to church leaders from one of the greatest disciple-martyrs of the ancient church. Perhaps we need to listen in a fresh way to those words.

That is precisely what this book is all about, listening to those precious final words of Paul in a fresh way, helping you to hear them just as the leaders of Ephesus first heard them; enabling you to apply them to your own life and ministry.

MICHAEL CARD
Christian singer-songwriter, musician, and author—Franklin TN

Preface

"WHAT IS *THE MINISTRY WE NEED*?" The way we answer this question can be telling. Opinions abound, the church brims with pragmatic suggestions, and the world is always ready to put in its depraved two cents. In the end all that really matters is what God says and what He thinks as revealed in His Word. While other works focus on the activities of a minister (and this one will certainly do this), here we will focus on *who* the minister is – and the character and content of his ministry. Knowing what you believe shapes how you live and, in this case, how you minister. Through Scripture, the authors will show the biggest temptations for the minister may be in doing things that are not necessarily ministry, or ministry's best.

This book offers encouragement, pastoral exhortation, and a needed reminder to solidify our focus regarding "the calling you have received (Eph 4:1)" during a time when ministers are walking away from the ministry or staying in the ministry and being rendered ineffective due to a loss of vision, purpose, focus or motivation. Ministers fail in ministry or leave the ministry altogether for numerous reasons. Most recently, the new reality of COVID-19 has significantly compounded the difficulty of ministry. Barna Group (research specialists) reports, regarding the pandemic, "Week after week, we're seeing the beginning signs of this crisis taking a longer-term toll on pastors, on their families and on their people" (March 31, 2020). Point is, if we as ministers do not focus on our high calling from God we may suffer loss of direction, or worse, loss of ministry. According to Thom Rainer "the pandemic really just exacerbated trends already in place" (Blog—*Six Reasons Your Pastor Is About to Quit*, August 31, 2020).

To every minister who is spiritually drifting or knows of one who is considering leaving the ministry and the church behind, this book is an attempt to encourage and empower them to re-embrace their calling and live out the ministry so desperately needed by the church. Each of the following chapters includes real life stories and insights from those who have faithfully walked the *ministry we need*, in order that fellow ministers might find inspiration to continue to serve faithfully themselves.

While analysis and diagnosis are certainly necessary, remedy is paramount – hence *the ministry we need*! One can only find the answer to that *need* in the sacred Scriptures. Outside of Christ, there is no greater ministry example in the New Testament than the Apostle Paul. Whether we are just needing a reminder, a refresher, or a complete reorientation of our approach to ministry we should all be able to receive help from a look at the ministry of the Apostle Paul as he passionately describes it in his parting instructions to the Ephesian elders (Acts 20:17–38).

Acts 20:17–18 (*A Consistent Ministry*) is the focus of chapter 1. Over time we can become comfortable in the routine of ministry. Our preaching, our focus, our lifestyle cannot be subject to the winds of change in the theological landscape, the "spirit of the age," or even the day-to-day difficulties of life. We must begin to think of our ministries not in terms of frustrating monotony but of faithful steadiness and reliability, hence *a consistent ministry*. Chapters 2–3 cover Acts 20:19. First (*A Humble Ministry*), God chose to describe his ministers as shepherds. Humility defines and characterizes the shepherd. An arrogant shepherd is an oxymoron. Pride incessantly pulls at us in every area of ministry. We need a ministry that mirrors that of Jesus, *a humble ministry*. Then (*A Ready Ministry*), Scripture commands us to "be ready in season and out of season" (2 Tim 4:2). We minister during the flourishing times of joy and peace, but ministry should also flourish in the face of tears, trials, and plots among other things – what we need is *a ready ministry*.

A Bold Ministry is the topic of chapter 4 dealing with Acts 20:20. Boldness, for the minister, is not always natural and he should never take it for granted. Absence of boldness in ministry makes us feeble, fearful, and indifferent. Because the Spirit lives within the minister there may be reasons for our lack of boldness but there is never any good excuse. What we need in a day of fear is *a bold ministry*. Chapter 5 (*A Gospel-centered Ministry*) covers Acts 20:21. Ministry can be many things to many people, but what we need is a ministry based on and grounded in the Lord Jesus Christ, therefore a *gospel-centered ministry*. If not, then it does not really qualify as *Christian* ministry. This is not just theory, but also practice. The subject for chapter 6 (Acts 20:22–23) is *A Spirit-led Ministry*. The authors will reveal the necessity of the Spirit's work and vital presence in the life of the man of God. *Spirit led* conjures up all sorts of images, some biblical,

Preface

some unbiblical. What we need is a ministry based not on experience or opinion but one fixed, dependent, and grounded on the revealed Holy Spirit of Scripture, therefore a *Spirit-led ministry*.

A Mission-minded Ministry (Acts 20:24) is the aim of chapter 7. The Great Commission mandates that we *make disciples*, therefore we are always "on mission." From the moment of salvation until its glorious culmination our ministries have a goal – to fulfill the glorious calling we have received from the Lord. We need a *mission-minded ministry* for we are either mission-minded or a mission field. Next, will be *A Blameless and Complete Ministry* (Acts 20:25–27). Sadly today, many who occupy a pulpit stand accused of actions, activities, and attitudes that bring reproach to Christ and His church – in a moment, a ministry can face ruin, therefore what we need is *a ministry that is blameless and complete* from start to finish. Chapter 9 will give attention to *A Vigilant Ministry* (Acts 20:28–31). This is a treacherous world; sadly, the church is not immune. There is a constant battle for the souls of men within the church because of wolves appearing as shepherds and hellish fare appearing as divine sustenance. We need a *vigilant ministry* always alert, ready, and willing to pay the price for truth.

The final three sections will involve the last seven verses of Acts 20. *A Dependent Ministry* (Acts 20:32) begins this segment (chapter 10). Ministers depend on many things – some good, some not so much. Paul tells them that their only hope, to which he commits them, is one that finds itself in God and His grace … they are completely dependent upon God for everything both now and in eternity. God and His grace are both *efficient* and *sufficient* for the minister and his ministry's well-being. What we desperately need is a *dependent* ministry. Then, Acts 20:33–35 will emphasize *A Content & Hardworking Ministry*. Pulpits today are full of unhappy and discontented fellows always looking for the next "big-thing." The call to ministry and the call to work hard are not mutually exclusive, they go hand in hand. The ministry needed today is a *content and hard-working* ministry. Finally, chapter 12 highlights *A Relational Ministry* (Acts 20:36–38). Some pastors keep a safe distance from their congregations, fearing transparency and vulnerability. The minister that knows his congregants well, will do so by allowing them to know him well. We must have a *relational* ministry to minister well.

Put Your Hand to the Plow will offer a concluding exhortation to the work. It will allow for a final personal encouragement from each of the three authors and will supply both biblical and practical advice. A recap of

Preface

all facets of *the ministry we need*, with a look to the future and the minister's judgment when we stand one day before the Great Shepherd (Heb 13:20). In this book, the authors will: 1) reveal the richness and depth of God's Word by drawing from a singular biblical passage (Acts 20:17–38), while retaining both exegetical and applicational integrity, 2) show some of the dangerous pitfalls of ministry such as arrogance, discontentment, laziness, walking in flesh, and the failure to finish well, 3) offer biblical and theological reasoning for their conclusions, 4) provide practical insight for the real world, 5) provide a sense of urgency and tenacity to "the calling which we have received," 6) provide not only a remedy for what ails the minister, but preventatives to keep him well, 7) present 12 examples of God working that principle out in real-life ministry examples through personal pastoral testimony and biography of faithful ministers, 8) present 12 focused prayers so the servant of God may zero in on a characteristic or truth he might obtain and/or confess where he has fallen short, and 9) show some of the glorious wonders of ministry such as being bold for the Lord, having the Spirit lead you, being on mission with God, having a complete ministry leading to the ultimate, "Well done, good and faithful servant" (Matt 25:21).

Our desire is to encourage God's servants, as well as those who may have veered off course. Our hope is that you will find refreshment and encouragement to press *in* and press *on* in your calling. To those who are training for pastoral ministry and those who train them our hope is that you will see this as a tool you can use, a companion work for teaching homiletics, practical theology, local church ministries, or leadership.

Acknowledgments

(Jeremy) To LouAnn, my dearest earthly treasure. To my beautiful children, Jeremiah, SaraBeth, EllaGrace, Micah, and KatieJoy. Finally, to my wonderful church family, Eastwood Baptist Church in Bowling Green, Kentucky, for the time you have given me to work on this project and for allowing me the amazing privilege of being your pastor, I truly love you.

(Jordan) To my wife Julia, and to my children, Josiah, Elijah, and Addison, you are a gift of our Savior's marvelous grace to my own soul and to all who know you. May our Lord shower His blessings on you always. To Hillcrest Baptist Church of Nederland, Texas, it is the joy of my life to have been assigned by our Lord to preach and teach His Word to you. May the Lord make your testimony sound forth through to the nations for His glory.

(Tony) To Terrie, best friend, love of my life and precious gift from God. To my children, Jeremy, Heather, and Jordan, you are my heritage, my reward, and my arrows (Ps 127:3–4). To their spouses, LouAnn, Robbie, and Julia, you are the helper I prayed that God would give my child. To my grandchildren, Jeremiah, McKinnley, SaraBeth, Bailey, EllaGrace, Emmerson, Paisley, Micah, Josiah, Elijah, Deacon, KatieJoy, Piper, and Addy Jo, you are my crown. To the church I shepherd, Southside Baptist, Bowie, Texas, it is my pleasure to feed you.

We would also like to thank all those who endorsed this effort and Michael Card who graciously supplied the Foreword. To Terrie Rogers and Lisa Dunn who painstakingly edited and offered stylistic suggestions. To Wipf & Stock for publishing this effort. Finally, to our Lord and Savior Jesus Christ who saved us, called us to preach, and continues to use us. We entered this journey with much fear and trepidation, but Your grace allowed us to understand that You did not give us a spirit of timidity, but of power, love, and discipline (2 Tim 1:7). We are truly blessed men.

Abbreviations

BDAG	Walter Bauer, Frederick W. Danker, W. F. Arndt, and F. W. Gingrich. *Greek- English Lexicon of the New Testament and Other Early Christian Literature.* 3rd ed. Chicago: University of Chicago Press, 2000.
CNTC	*Calvin's New Testament Commentaries.* 12 vols. Edited by David W. Torrance and Thomas F. Grand Rapids: Eerdmans, 1990s.
EBC	*The Expositor's Bible Commentary.* 12 vols. Edited by Frank Gaebelein. Grand Rapids: Zondervan, 1976–1992.
ERLC	The Ethics and Religious Liberty Commission of the Southern Baptist Convention, Nashville Tennessee.
HNTC	Holman New Testament Commentary. 12 vols. Edited by Max Anders. Nashville: Holman Reference, 1998–2000.
Louw–Nida	Louw and Nida, eds. Greek-English Lexicon of the New Testament: Based on Semantic Domains. New York: United Bible Societies, 1996.
NAC	*The New American Commentary.* 42 vols. Edited by E. Ray Clendenen, Kenneth A. Matthews, David S. Dockery. Nashville: Broadman, 1991–2020.
SBC	Southern Baptist Convention
SBTC	Southern Baptist of Texas Convention
SBTS	The Southern Baptist Theological Seminary, Louisville Kentucky.

Chapter 1

A Consistent Ministry

> *"The good minister is to be hard at work that he might pass all the way to the finish line and that others, by grace, might join him there."*
>
> — ALISTAIR BEGG[1] —

Acts 20:17–18 "Now from Miletus he sent to Ephesus and called the elders of the church to come to him. And when they came to him, he said to them: "You yourselves know *how I lived among you the whole time from the first day that I set foot in Asia* . . ."

Commentary

Acts 20:13–16 gives the reader a detailed look at Paul's travel itinerary and immediately precedes the account of Acts 20:17–38. Just a few verses earlier in Acts 20:16 Theophilus is told the Apostle and his companions had intentionally sailed past Ephesus without stopping. As Paul arrives in Miletus, a coastal town approximately 30 miles from Ephesus, he "sent to Ephesus and called" in which *metekalesato*, translated "called," carries an authoritative emphasis. This would have certainly led Theophilus, and should lead us,

---

1. Begg, "Good Servant of Christ Jesus," 47:22.

to understand both the importance of the moment to Paul and the solemn nature of this final meeting and its content.[2]

The Apostle Paul began his speech to the Ephesian elders by emphatically reminding them of the consistent nature of his ministry the entire length of time he was with them.[3] This constancy that marked his ministry is so well known by the Ephesian church's leadership that Paul has no problem holding them accountable for this knowledge regarding his three years of ministry among them. According to Puritan pastor, Matthew Henry:

> He appeared from the first day they knew him to be a man that aimed not only to do well, but to do good, wherever he came. He was a man that was consistent with himself, and all of a piece; take him where you would he was the same at all seasons, he did not turn with the wind nor change with the weather, but was uniform like a die, which, throw it which way you will, lights on a square side.[4]

The Apostle's emphasis here is to remind the Ephesian elders of the *nature* of his ministry among them ("how I lived") the entire time he was with them.

> What Paul wishes to remind them of is not merely his message but his manner of life, for he is instructing fellow leaders who must themselves take up the mantle of setting examples for others. Paul insists on the consistency of his behavior—it was the same from the very first day he set foot in the province of Asia until now when he is leaving it.[5]

Paul's manner of life in Ephesus over the span of three years was something of which they were acutely aware, and he was quick to point out as a clear example the steady nature of his ministry among them. The Apostle's daily living and ministry practice among the Ephesian believers was clearly consistent for the duration of his time among them.

> Ministry Principle: there will always be the temptation in ministry to be distracted by other pursuits, whether they be notoriety, accolades, or hobbies. However, we need to pursue faithfully and

---

2. Peterson, *Acts of the Apostles*, 563. For further explanation as to the forceful nature of this calling see Louw–Nida, 423.
3. Polhill, *NAC, Acts*, 424.
4. Henry, *Commentary on the Whole Bible*, 2156.
5. Witherington, *Acts of the Apostles*, 616.

daily the calling the Lord has placed upon our lives as ministers, in other words, we must have *a consistent ministry*.

A Portrait of a Consistent Ministry

While this book is certainly applicable to pastoral ministry, primarily, it applies to other areas of ministry within the kingdom of God as well. From the time I (Jeremy) was a young man, I heard stories of Dr. H. Leroy Metts, the now retired Senior Distinguished Professor Emeritus of Greek and New Testament at Criswell College in Dallas, Texas. Dr. Metts's ministry of teaching and preaching the Word of God has spanned decades, with the last 45 years of his ministry being in the classroom. Dr. Metts has spent these years clearly and consistently teaching scores of young ministers how to handle the Word faithfully. During these years of ministry in the academic community he has quietly pursued nothing but excellence in the study of the New Testament and faithfulness to the One who has revealed Himself through it. "When other people devoted their energies to writing or gaining a reputation or using the classroom as a springboard to a large pulpit and a large salary, Roy gave his life to the exegesis of God's Word and [preaching] the Gospel of the Kingdom before the Kingdom was ever cool."[6]

It is no secret among those who have had Dr. Metts in the classroom or have been around his teaching ministry that he is faithful and consistent in his ministry. There were many days when I would arrive at the college early in the morning to unlock everything and Dr. Metts was already there preparing for 7 a.m. Greek tutoring sessions for any of his students who needed a little extra help (of which I was certainly one!). There were semesters when Dr. Metts also taught a late block class from 7 to 9:30 p.m. on the same days he had 7 a.m. tutoring and he was usually the last one to leave. It was, and is, a well-known fact for those privileged to know him that he is always there, not just as a professor, but to pray for anyone in need and to invest in your life personally. My wife gave birth to our son at Baylor Hospital, a couple of blocks from Criswell College in Dallas, Texas, during midterms. After a Greek Exegetical Syntax Exam, Dr. Metts grabbed me by the arm and said, "Now, for something truly important . . . let's go see that new son of yours." On a 30-degree February day in Dallas, Dr. Metts walked

---

6. Staff, "40-Year Criswell Prof Honored," para. 3.

the two blocks with me to the hospital, hugged my wife, held my newborn son, and went back to give another exam.

Now you might be asking yourself, "What does this have to do with being consistent in ministry?" and, if you are not familiar with Dr. Metts, your question is not outrageous. You might think, "It is not uncommon for someone to minister to someone like that" or "Maybe Dr. Metts is just really close to them and felt compelled to do this because of their relationship." However, this is how he is with everyone, this is how he was when he started teaching at Criswell College in the 1970's, and it is how he is even now. There is no doubt his amazing intellect, his obvious gift from the Lord in the areas of New Testament Studies and Greek, and his unwavering passion for the Word of God and the Person and work of Jesus Christ have affected countless ministers and their churches through them. However, for those who know him and those to whom he has ministered, the things that leave the most lasting impression of Dr. Leroy Metts is his care, his willingness to always be there to lend a helping hand or ear, and the fact that he has been consistently that in many lives for many years.

You Must Be Consistent in Your Preaching

We have been given a blessing in the book of Acts because the passage to which we have been looking is an account of the Apostle Paul regarding his ministry among the Ephesians. However, the even greater blessing can be found in the previous chapter of Acts in which Luke himself gives an outside view of the Apostle's ministry in Ephesus. In Acts 19:8 we are told, "And [Paul] entered the synagogue and for three months spoke boldly, reasoning and persuading them about the Kingdom of God." The account given in chapter 19 serves to confirm Paul's testimony in chapter 20 and shows us clearly how Paul ministered consistently, specifically about his preaching ministry.

Preaching Boldly

In the first three months Paul was with the Ephesians he continued the practice of preaching in the local synagogue which was his customary practice on his first two missionary journeys.[7] In Acts 19:8 Luke states that

---

7. Larkin, *Acts*, 274.

A Consistent Ministry

Paul *"spoke boldly"* among those gathered in the synagogue in Ephesus. The word, *eparrēsiazeto*, translated in the ESV as "he was speaking boldly" can also be understood as speaking "freely, openly, or fearlessly" and describes an act of declaration in which the speaker is not concerned by the negative outcomes that could accompany the message.[8] Paul spoke openly and without concern of reprisal and this approach is still just as needed today. In a culture, and even a church culture, that desires ministers who are careful to never offend or upset with the message of the truth, our ministries should be known for bold preaching. While we should always desire to be compassionate and caring, we must never believe the false narrative that compassion for people and the truth of Scripture are, somehow, diametrically opposed to one another. In fact, declaring the Word of God and accurately applying it to issues of the day, with boldness, is the most caring thing a minister can do . . . it is the ministry the people of God need.

There are many voices today calling the preacher to "give the people what they want" so that we might increase the church's appeal to the community or her attendance on any given weekend. But this is nothing new and was an issue the Apostle Paul dealt with even when he ministered to the church in Corinth. Human wisdom tells us today that the church needs to smooth out the message of the Scriptures so as to not offend people and give them what they are looking for so they feel the gospel is relevant to their daily life and so the messages they hear will satisfy their felt needs and scratch them where they itch. While it may seem wise to change our preaching to appeal to people so they will be drawn to the church, this is the exact opposite of the approach Paul describes in 1 Corinthians 1:21–23, "For since, in the wisdom of God, the world did not know God through wisdom, it pleased God through the folly of what we preach to save those who believe. For Jews demand signs and Greeks seek wisdom, but we preach Christ crucified, a stumbling block to Jews and folly to Gentiles . . . ." The simple truth is that the Apostle Paul describes his approach as one that did not give the people what they wanted but, instead, a ministry that boldly declared to the people what they actually needed, not just what they felt they needed.

As ministers, we preach God's message to the people. A minister who shirks responsibility, one who shifts the message in the face of so-called *church growth principles*, or one who shrinks before the demands of the culture and preaches what people want to hear, making his preaching more

---

8. BDAG, 782.

attractional and less *convictional*, has forgotten the first half of this truth. While we certainly preach a message *to* people, we also preach a message *from* God. Therefore, God is the origin of the message preached, and the minister is simply the vessel of the message preached. This requires him to boldly declare His message without shirking, shifting, or shrinking in his calling. Ministers are called to preach the Word boldly and give the people what God says they need and not what they think they need.

Preaching Reasonably

During his time in Ephesus, Luke not only tells us *how* Paul spoke to the Ephesians but *what* he did in his preaching ministry. In Acts 19:8, we read that Paul spoke boldly to his listeners, *reasoning* with them. The word translated "reasoning" (*dialegomenos*) can be defined as "an instructional discourse that frequently includes exchange of opinions."[9] This description makes it clear Paul was in the practice of explaining issues and answering questions in his preaching ministry. Paul's preaching ministry was certainly one of bold declaration, but it was simultaneously a ministry of clear explanation.

In an age prevalent with competing ideas, it is important we remember it is incumbent upon those who minister the Word that we engage the reigning worldviews of the day. The truth of Scripture engages and overthrows the supposed wisdom of the culture, and we must minister in such a way that we present the Scriptures not as one clear opinion among many but as the truth of God that stands superior to any and every other opinion. This concept of "reasoning" from the Scriptures was a constant throughout the entirety of the Apostle Paul's ministry from Thessalonica (Acts 17:2), to Athens (Acts 17:17), to Corinth (Acts 18:4), to Ephesus in both the synagogue (Acts 19:8) and the Hall of Tyrannus (Acts 19:9), to Troas (Acts 20:7, 9), and before Felix in Caesarea (Acts 24:25). As we follow the example of the Apostle Paul, we should not fail to show our people the reasonable nature of the Word of God.

---

9. BDAG, 232.

Preaching Persuasively

In Acts 19:8, Luke also recounts Paul's preaching ministry as having a goal of convincing the listeners. We are told Paul spoke boldly, showing the Ephesians the reasonable nature of his message and he did this with the goal of "*persuading*" them. This act of *'persuading'* (*peithōn*) meant the Apostle was moving to a decision with the goal of having the Ephesians "come to a particular point of view or course of action."[10] Paul's example shows us his desire to bring his listeners to a place of belief or action which required them to change course.

As ministers our calling is not to simply transfer information about God from His Word but to persuade people of the veracity of the message so that they are changed in mind and action by it. As ministers declare the Word of God, it is essential we move beyond an instructional discourse and realize, "Persuasion is necessary because all Scripture is counter-intuitive to the minds, emotions, and wills of the world's lied-to people."[11] Persuasion in preaching cannot be excluded because of the actual spiritual needs of the listeners to have their beliefs and actions changed by God, through His Word to combat the contrary nature of their thinking, actions, and the wisdom of the sin-broken world in which they live. As ministers of the gospel, the Apostle Paul's example in Ephesus shows us our preaching must be consistently bold, reasonable, and persuasive.

You Must Be Consistent in Your Focus

During the Apostle Paul's ministry in Ephesus, described in Acts 19:8, we are not only told *how* he preached ('boldly'), and *what* he did while preaching ('reasoning and persuading'), but we are also told *what* he preached, the content or focus of his message. We are told in the synagogue at Ephesus, for a period of three months, the sole focus of Paul's message was 'the kingdom of God.' Paul's message was no different than the message found on the lips of Jesus (Mark 1:15, Luke 4:43, Acts 1:3), the message Jesus gave His disciples to preach (Luke 9:2, 10:9), or the message of the early church (Acts 8:12).

Our job is to proclaim the Kingdom of God boldly, reasoning and persuading, to the people. The message of the Kingdom of God is that while

---

10. BDAG, 791.
11. Eclov, "Persuasion in Preaching," lines 2–4.

our sin-sick humanity seeks to live according to our own rules, the true King of all things has rightful claim over the universe, humanity, history, and our personal lives. The message of the Kingdom of God is that we owe our complete allegiance to Jesus Christ and must submit to His rule over our wills, emotions, thoughts, and actions. Therefore, the message of the Kingdom of God is a message that affects every aspect of our lives and changes our approach to everything from our beliefs about the nature of eternity, to our understanding of forgiveness, to the way we manage money. This means our singular focus is to consistently show how the Kingdom of God, and King Jesus, affect everything about the lives of His listeners. The temptation to focus on many different topics and seeking to appeal to people, can be great but our singular focus as ministers of the gospel is to bring the message of the Kingdom of God to bear consistently, boldly, reasonably, and persuasively in the lives of our hearers.

Over time, we can become comfortable in the routine of ministry, and not in a good way. As our daily tasks are so similar and the focus and purpose of our lives is always the same, we can grow so familiar and at-ease in what we do that we begin to slack in the areas of preaching, mission, and lifestyle. We must begin to think of our ministries not in terms of frustrating monotony but of faithful consistency. Our preaching, our mission/focus, and our lifestyles should be faithfully consistent. Our preaching, our focus, our lifestyle cannot be subject to the winds of change in the theological landscape, the *spirit of the age*, or even the day-to-day difficulties of life. While we must always be authentic and not stroll through life like everything is always fine, we must be an example of faithful consistency to those we have been called to guide, showing them that a faithful, bold, present, authentic life can be lived for Christ in this ever-changing world.

> 1 Corinthians 4:1–2 "This is how one should regard us, as servants of Christ and stewards of the mysteries of God. Moreover, it is required of stewards that they be found faithful."
>
> Prayer Point: Lord, forgive *me* for where *I* have lacked faithfulness to the ministry and where *I* have failed to be a good steward of the calling You have entrusted to *me*. *My* desire is to be consistent in *my* ministry recognizing *my* calling is not to fame or fortune but faithfulness to You and the gospel. May the ministry You have given *me* be marked by bold, reasonable, and persuasive preaching as *I* remain faithful to the message of the kingdom of God as *my* singular focus.

Chapter 2

A Humble Ministry

"Every good thing in the Christian life grows in the soil of humility. Without humility, every virtue and every grace withers."

— JOHN PIPER[1] —

Acts 20:19a *". . . serving the Lord with all humility . . ."*

Commentary

In the first two verses of Paul's farewell speech to the Ephesian elders, in Acts 20:17–18, the Apostle calls his audience to remember how he ministered among them for the entirety of the three years he was with them. After this introductory statement, Paul begins to explain the manner of his ministry for his tenure in Ephesus. The longest tenured stay of the Apostle's ministry, according to his own testimony, was marked by his *"serving"* (*douleuōn*). The use of this present active participle tells us this was his constant and continual approach to ministry while at the Ephesus. The word *douleuōn* describes the actions of one who performs "the duties of a slave . . . [one who] acts or conduct[s] oneself as one in total service to transcendent beings, especially in expressions relating to God or Jesus Christ as recipients of undivided allegiance."[2] So, Paul is describing something

---

1. Piper, "Greatness, Humility, Servanthood," 28:42.
2. BDAG, 259.

beyond simply doing a few things for someone else; instead he is telling his listeners that his ministry was marked by complete and total obedience, as a slave has no self-determination when it comes to fulfilling his calling. In this short section it is important to note that, while Paul was ministering to the Ephesian church, he specifically tells us that he was serving "the Lord". While his ministry was marked by serving, the object of his service was the Lord. As we have seen, the word translated "serving" can be understood as the relationship between "slave and master".[3] Paul claims this as his identity throughout the New Testament as he refers to himself continually as a "*doulōs*" or "slave" (Rom 1:1, Gal 1:10, Phil 1:1, Titus 1:1). Therefore, Paul's description of his ministry was one of complete servitude to the Lord alone.

In this short statement where the Apostle Paul describes *what* he did (serving) and *who* he served (the Lord), he then tells us the nature of his service whereby declaring he was serving the Lord "*meta pasēs tapeinophrosynēs*," translated "with all humility". This characteristic is one the Apostle sees as an absolute necessity, not just in ministry, but in the Christian life. This truth is made evident by Paul repeatedly in the New Testament, whether he is telling believers that humility is a distinctive characteristic of those who "walk in a manner worthy" (Eph 4:2), or how we might have the mind of Christ and "count others more significant than [ourselves]" (Phil 2:3), or how, as God's children, we are to put on "humility" among other essential qualities (Col 3:12). The Apostle Paul's ministry in Ephesus was not about making a name for himself but about serving and exalting the One who had his allegiance.

> Ministry Principle: certain aspects of ministry, and our own weaknesses, can leave us open to pride and arrogance. Therefore, we need to be consumed by the One we serve, remembering that He alone is worthy of all glory, honor, and praise . . . *we need a humble ministry.*

A Portrait of a Humble Ministry

I (Jeremy) was 26 years old and had become the pastor of a rural church in Texas just one year prior. I had been everything from a Missions Intern to Minister of Students, but this was my very first pastorate. Now at that time I had already been preaching regularly for 13 years, had my bachelor's degree

---

3. Larkin, *Acts*, 293.

in Biblical Studies and had just completed my master's degree. Basically, I had it all nailed down and I was well on my way. I mean, at that point I figured I had everything figured out for the most part and all I needed to do to gain respect was show people how much I knew about Scripture and how to preach it. In short, I was awesome, and I was simply waiting for everyone else to realize what I already knew to be true! Obviously, I never verbalized that and never admitted it to myself internally but looking back this is the sentiment ringing in my heart (and makes me cringe!).

However, that year something happened in my life that could be called a defining moment. While ministering at this small country church, in an area that is the dictionary definition of rural, I met an extremely Godly man named Don. Don and his family began visiting the church shortly after I was called there and joined soon after that. Don is probably 20 years my senior and came to know Christ later in life. Simply put, he is a man who can be called "a pastor's friend," supportive, encouraging, completely trustworthy, and always willing to be a sounding board.

Don is a scientist professionally and is extremely interested in the aspects of Creationism and Intelligent Design and has been involved in reading, going to conferences, and building relationships in that community for some time. This particular year, Don determined he and his family wanted to bless me for Pastor Appreciation month by taking me to a large national conference on Intelligent Design. I was overwhelmed to receive such a kind and thoughtful gift from a church member. The conference proved to be interesting and enlightening, but the lunch break was the highlight of the entire trip. This lunch was not a highlight because it was a particularly intriguing breakout session or a thought-provoking Q&A. In fact, the lunch consisted of sitting in a chair across from one other eating a boxed lunch in a conference room. As we were eating, we discussed everything from family life to particular styles of music in worship services. I spent a portion of our lunch bemoaning certain aspects of our church and telling him I believed if the church would just listen to my awesome ideas, everything would be fixed.

Then the moment came when Don looked up from his meal and said, "I have been praying for a while about how and when to say this. Can I tell you something as a friend and someone who cares about you deeply?" During that split-second I thought "He is probably going to tell me how much he appreciates my ministry and about why he wanted to bless me with this conference." So, I said, "Yes!" However, he looked me in my eye and, truly, in the most sincere, heartfelt, and loving way said, "You are an extremely arrogant and prideful man." To be perfectly honest, this was not the first time someone had pointed out something about me they didn't like but this was different. This friend went out of his way to show his love, respect, and concern for me before he made his statement. I was crushed to the deepest part of my being. Even as I write this, his words resonate deep within and cause a pain that is, to this day, beneficial for my soul which is still prone to wander down the path of pride.

We spent the rest of the day together at the conference and there were many great speakers and presentations, but I don't remember any of them. All I could hear were his words echoing in my ears. God used that moment in my life to speak truth into my heart and I can say, without reservation, I am thankful to the Lord for the grace He showed me through Don. That day changed the way I see myself and God has continually used it to reorient me when I am in danger of allowing pride to creep in.

Criticism and, sadly, even condemnation can be prevalent in pastoral ministry, but God showed His grace in bringing me a brother who was willing to be obedient to the Lord and follow Paul's admonition in Ephesians 4:15 by " . . . [speaking] the truth in love." Pride is not a "ministry issue" it is a "heart issue" and as such it is absolutely vital that we understand the essential nature of humility in our lives and ministry.

Humble Because of the Lowly Nature of Our Calling

In following the example of Paul, we can see humility should be a given simply due to the nature of our identification as servants/slaves of a great Master. As God's servants, we are completely subservient to Him; therefore, any action, accomplishment, or accolade is entirely for His glory alone and we can lay claim to nothing. This truth should bring into stark realization that even the high calling of ministry is only high because of the One we serve, the One we proclaim. Regardless of what praise or honor may be given to us by men, when we remember our position of grace before the Lord, our ministries should be attended by humility because of our lowly position as servants of the Most High.

Who We Are

Since we are to be identified as servants then we must recognize we ultimately owe even *who we are* to the Lord. Now, we know all believers are granted spiritual gifts when we come to faith in Christ (1 Cor 12:4–7), however, we can be tempted to think that other aspects of what we do, as ministers, are because we have worked hard and have cultivated those things. While it is certainly true that we must work hard to develop the areas in which we are deficient we can never claim these as our gifts either. Our abilities, even those that have taken years of work and discipline, are gifts from the Lord because any capacity in which we must learn, grow, attain, or achieve can't be attributed to our own strength. Pride and arrogance have no place in our ministries or in our hearts because the praise for every good thing regarding *who* we are and *what* we may be able to do can only be attributed to the good grace of our Master.

Where We Are

Have you arrived? Are you pastoring a prominent church? Are you held in high esteem by the people of your congregation? Are you well known in your community? Or do you find yourself in the lowliest of positions, one of the smallest churches, or in an out-of-the-way rural community? In whatever position you may find yourself, God alone retains the glory for your place in ministry. Regardless of where we may find ourselves ministering, all positions garner the same glory, have the same honor, and deserve the same praise. However, because we are servants, all the glory, honor, and praise belong to the One who has graced us with the tremendous privilege to serve Him. Since we are not able to claim any glory for where we find ourselves in ministry, whether today, or in the future, it makes no difference *where we are*, we must serve our merciful Lord in humility.

What We Achieve

Much like the position in which we might find ourselves, our achievements, whether ministerially, academically, or otherwise can be attended by a temptation to "think of [ourselves] more highly than [we] ought to think" (Rom 12:3). Did you get invited to speak at *that* conference, to write *that* journal article, preach at *that* church, review *that* book, speak on *that* podcast, did you earn *that* degree, did you get *that* title, did you have *that* many in attendance, or did your church give *that* much to missions? Each of these achievements can be wonderful things but whether the answer to any of those questions is "Yes," or will be "Yes" in the future, we must keep the proper perspective. Just as any ability we may have or any position we may hold, anything we may achieve in ministry must not inflate our own view of ourselves simply because we are servants and *what we achieve* belongs solely to our loving King.

Humble Because of the Supreme Object of Our Calling

In this farewell address to the Ephesian elders the Apostle Paul is certainly describing his ministry in Ephesus and his character as he ministered but he ultimately identifies the object of his service and ministry. While it is obvious the Ephesian people were the human beneficiaries of his work, the Lord Himself was the One on which Paul's gaze was set. As servants of the Lord, our calling consists entirely of obeying *His* commands, following *His* guidance, ministering to *His* church, sharing *His* gospel, and preaching and teaching *His* Word. As His servants, we are called to give our entire lives to His service, for the glory of His name, and we must never take or expect any glory for ourselves. We must view ourselves exactly the way Jesus described all His servants in His parable found in Luke 17:7–10:

> Will any one of you who has a servant plowing or keeping sheep say to him when he has come in from the field, 'Come at once and recline at table'? Will he not rather say to him, 'Prepare supper for me, and dress properly, and serve me while I eat and drink, and afterward you will eat and drink'? Does he thank the servant because he did what was commanded? So you also, when you have done all that you were commanded, say, 'We are unworthy servants; we have only done what was our duty.'

When we spend our lives serving the Lord, with the gifts and abilities He has given us, in the places He has blessed us to minister, and achieving all that He has given us the ability to do we can only be identified as "unworthy servants" because we have fulfilled our calling, or duty, which is to serve Him with our entire selves.

Pride occurs when our view of God begins to shrink, and our view of self inflates. An ever-increasing view of God and His majesty is one of the best ways to combat pride in the human heart. As we revel in God's divine glory our own vainglory fades into the distance because either God is going to occupy the throne in the center of my existence or I am, both cannot. John the Baptizer declared, referencing his ministry in relation to Jesus, in John 3:30, "He must increase, but I must decrease." In context, John was referring to the fact that he had come to "Prepare the way of the Lord . . . " (Matt 3:3) and now that Jesus had come his ministry was no longer needed. However, John's sentiment rings true in relation to pride in the human heart as well. As we combat pride in our own hearts and our vision of God increases, our view of self will decrease. Therefore, a daily, intentional, and genuine magnification of God will subsequently lead to the destruction of pride in our hearts. As we continue to die to ourselves daily, consistently looking to destroy our pride, then, and only then, are we *"serving the Lord with all humility."*

> Psalms 34:1–3 "I will bless the Lord at all times; His praise shall continually be in my mouth. My soul makes its boast in the Lord; let the humble hear and be glad. Oh, magnify the Lord with me, and let us exalt His name together!"
>
> Prayer Point: Lord, forgive *me* for where *I* have exhibited pride and arrogance in *my* life and ministry. Father, grant *me* the grace to worship You daily and have an ever-increasing view of Your majesty. Lord, may *I* daily remember that *I* am an "unworthy servant" of a gloriously loving, gracious, and merciful Father.

Chapter 3

A Ready Ministry

"It is doubtful whether God can bless a man greatly until He has hurt him deeply."

— A.W. TOZER[1] —

Acts 20:19 " . . . and with tears and with trials that happened to me through the plots of the Jews . . . "

Commentary

Thus far, in Acts 20:17–19a, Luke has given us an account of Paul's farewell address to the elders of the church in Ephesus. The Apostle Paul has described the nature of his ministry during his time with the Ephesian believers, reminding them that he served the Lord, and his service of ministry was attended by humility. However, in Acts 20:19, there are two other aspects of Paul's ministry that were prevalent during his time there. The Ephesian elders are called to remember that his ministry was accompanied by *"dakryōn,"* translated "tears". There was an aspect of personal suffering and pain that was an apparent part of the ministry of Paul, so much so that he was able to call it to the elders's remembrance. The Apostle's ministry approach was certainly personal, "For he shed the *tears* of a tender heart."[2]

1. Tozer, *Root of the Righteous*, 165.
2. Larkin, *Acts*, 293.

A Ready Ministry

Tears could certainly be a response to joy or happiness but are more often associated with pain or sorrow, as seems to be the context in this passage. In the words of Derek Thomas:

> Paul's ministry had cost him emotionally and continued to do so. His involvement was not out of a mere sense of professionalism. His activity was more than a mere routine. He had become involved in the work on a personal level . . . There ought to be the closest bond between a pastor and his congregation.[3]

While it could certainly be conjectured that Paul's ministry in Ephesus had its high points, especially considering he established the church there which was, no doubt, preceded and followed by scores of people coming to faith in Jesus Christ. However, Paul chooses to highlight the "tears" as a well-known part of his ministry.

Not only was the Apostle Paul's ministry marked by his grief but, in a seemingly separate issue listed in verse 19, he experienced difficulty in the form of *"kai peirasmōn tōn symbantōn moi en tais epiboulais tōn Ioudaiōn"* which is translated "with trials that happened to me through the plots of the Jews." It is interesting that Paul calls the Ephesian elders to remember the trials he experienced from plots the Jews formed while with them. The narrative account of his ministry in Ephesus in Acts (Acts 19:9) doesn't mention a specific plot of the Jews, however, the absence of any mention of a plot does not mean one didn't occur since this was a common occurrence during the entire ministry of the Apostle Paul during his missionary journeys. During his first missionary journey, we are told the gospel was spreading throughout the region of Antioch in Pisidia and the Jews incited the prominent people to persecute Paul and his companions and drive them out (Acts 13:50). After they were driven out of Antioch, Paul and his cohort travelled to Iconium and saw tremendous gospel fruit but then the Jews stirred up the Gentiles which led Paul and his friends to flee the city (Acts 14:2–7). Fleeing from Iconium, Paul began to preach the gospel in Lystra but the Jews from Antioch and Iconium showed up, began a mission of subversion, and ultimately stoned Paul, dragged him out of the city, believing they had killed him (Acts 14:19).[4] Sometime later, during

---

3. Thomas, *Acts*, 578.

4. It should be noted that after Paul and his ministry team were run out of Antioch in Pisidia under persecution, then fled Iconium under threat of being killed, and after being stoned and left for dead the Apostle and his companions, "When they had preached the gospel to that city [Derbe] and had made many disciples, they returned to Lystra and to

Paul's second missionary journey, he and Silas had many converts in Thessalonica, which angered the Jews, and the church sent Paul and Silas away by night (Acts 17:5-9). Fleeing in the night Paul and Silas began ministry in Berea, saw many come to faith in Christ, and the Jews from Thessalonica came to Berea and stirred up trouble for Paul causing the church there to send him away for his own safety (Acts 17:13). After ministering in Athens, Paul went to Corinth where the Jews strongly opposed him, and he turned to ministering to the Gentiles in that area (Acts 18:6). Paul's ministry in the regions of Macedonia and Achaia were for a period of a year and a half and then the Jews attacked Paul and brought him before the Gentile rulers (Acts 18:12-17). During Paul's third missionary journey, he arrived in Greece, but a plot was created by the Jews when he was about to sail to Syria, so he returned to Macedonia (Acts 20:3). We can clearly see the Apostle Paul's ministry had many amazing moments of gospel advance and work but the extreme persecution of those Jews who did not believe the message of Christ was his constant companion.

> Ministry Principle: there are certainly many wonderful and glorious aspects to the gospel ministry, however, we must be prepared for the necessary vulnerability as well as the certain difficulty and opposition we will encounter ... *we need a ready ministry.*

A Portrait of a Ready Ministry

The 1980's are known for many newsworthy events but in the evangelical world there may have been no more well-known movement than what became known as the Conservative Resurgence of the Southern Baptist Convention. During this time, the largest Protestant denomination in the world changed course from its decades long liberal theological drift to dropping anchor firmly in the harbor of theological conservatism. In the minds of many in the Southern Baptist Convention, there needed to be a shift within the convention's seminaries to see lasting change, not the least being the flagship seminary, the Southern Baptist Theological Seminary in Louisville, Kentucky.

Iconium and to Antioch." (Acts 14:21) Though he experienced great persecution in those places, even to the point of near martyrdom, he never ended the mission or strayed from his calling.

A Ready Ministry

In 1993 the Board of Trustees of Southern Seminary elected 33-year-old Dr. R. Albert Mohler, Jr. to be the 9th President. From the beginning, Dr. Mohler made his stance clear regarding the past theological direction of the seminary and where his strong conservative stand on the inerrancy of Scripture and his subsequent vision for the school would lead. Dr. Mohler's commitment to Southern being confessionally orthodox was met with immediate resistance from every direction within the seminary, from the student body to the overwhelming majority of the faculty. Because Southern was the flagship seminary of the convention, this resistance was reported far and wide. While Dr. Mohler stood firm, he was met daily with students protesting, refusing to acknowledge him at graduation ceremonies, carrying caskets around the seminary grounds no doubt lamenting what they saw as the death of Southern under his leadership. However, if this wasn't bad enough, in April of 1995, all but four of the seminary's faculty members passed a vote of "no confidence" in Dr. Mohler's leadership and delivered it to the board of trustees with the hope he would be removed.

While this is all history, and the board of trustees fully affirmed Dr. Mohler and his leadership, what we can learn from his example is as applicable today as it was in the past. It is difficult to overstate the impact Dr. Mohler has had on Southern Seminary and the Southern Baptist Convention, over these last almost 30 years. Scores of young men and women have been theologically prepared and sent out all over the world to churches, on mission, and in the public square to share the hope of Jesus Christ with a desperate world. Dr. Mohler has also affected countless listeners as he confronts cultural issues facing the church through his ministry, The Briefing. While these achievements are tremendous none of them would have happened had he not stood firm, as a champion of the faith, amid extreme opposition, holding fast to an unwavering commitment to the Word of God, the gospel of Jesus Christ, and theological orthodoxy.[5]

Leading in any ministry has always meant facing opposition or difficulty of some kind. To lead and to fulfill the calling of ministry means you will not escape hardship and resistance as you seek to be obedient to the One who has called you. If these things can't be avoided or escaped, then it means they must be understood and faced. As we face opposition, even persecution, in the gospel ministry we must be firmly planted in our

---

5. SBTS, "XXV: The Enduring Vision," entire video; SBTS, "Recovering a Vision," entire video; Aaron Hanbury, "Twenty Years and Counting," entire article.

convictions and fully prepared to grow through the hardship, we must not be surprised, we must be ready.

Cultivate A Broken Heart in Ministry

It is all too easy to grow callused and bitter in ministry, especially after an extended period at a particularly difficult pastorate or ministry assignment. However, we can never allow ourselves to become insensitive toward the people to whom we are called. To avoid becoming cold toward ministry, we must be willing as a matter of importance to seek the Lord that we might, through the power of the Holy Spirit, be broken over the right things, the same things that broke the heart of the Apostle Paul. While things may seem to come more naturally to some, we must be willing to cultivate and grow in any areas where we are deficient. In the New Testament, we are shown three areas that broke the heart of Paul and it should be our desire that our hearts are broken over these same things. These three areas drive the Apostle onward in ministry, even when faced with extreme hardship and opposition. As we have trouble in ministry, we can be ready to face it as we cry out to the Lord to break our hearts: over the lost, over sin within the church, and over the prevalence of false teaching that threatens to lead so many astray.

Broken Over Lostness

We are given deep insight into the depth of passion felt by the Apostle Paul by Paul himself in Romans 9:1-3. The previous chapter culminates in a well-known declaration, in 8:39, regarding the permanent nature of God's love and the inability of being or circumstance to separate us from that love found only in "Christ Jesus our Lord." Then we hear the broken heart of the Apostle Paul as he laments the lostness of Israel and declares:

> I am speaking the truth in Christ–I am not lying; my conscience bears me witness in the Holy Spirit–that *I have great sorrow and unceasing anguish in my heart*. For I could wish that I myself were accursed and cut off from Christ for the sake of my brothers, my kinsmen according to the flesh (Rom 9:1-3).

As the Apostle saw the lostness of the Jewish nation, he was overcome with "great sorrow and unceasing anguish in [his] heart." Paul has such a desire to see others come to faith in Christ, specifically his Jewish kinsmen, he is willing to give up his own eternal life with Christ if they would put their faith in Him. This is the cry of one who saw no amount of suffering, no amount of hardship, no amount of persecution he may incur as worse than the eternal damnation of those to whom he was called.

As ministers of the gospel, we are called to declare the unsearchable riches of Christ to those who do not believe so they might trust in Him alone for their eternal life. However, the task of preaching the Good News should be accompanied by a heart that is desperately broken over the lostness of those who hear us. Jesus Christ Himself showed us what it looked like to have a heart broken over the lost and their coming judgment. Even in relation to those directly perpetrating the persecution against Him in Luke 19:41–44 Jesus wept aloud, crying out "Would that you, even you, had known on this day the things that make for peace! But now they are hidden from your eyes." While there will certainly be difficult days and moments that push us to a breaking point in the ministry, if we will seek to cultivate hearts that are broken for the lost, we will be ready to endure the difficulty so we might see even one come to Christ by faith.

Broken Over Sinfulness

Even a cursory reading of both letters to the church in Corinth will show the Corinthian church had a serious, pervasive issue with sin within the church. The open debauchery and sexual sin being practiced was said to be repulsive even among non-believing pagans (1 Cor 5:1). The Corinthian church was openly rebuked by the Apostle Paul for allowing a man to live in sexual immorality with his stepmother and still minister and fellowship in the church without being called to righteousness and repentance (1 Cor 5:1–13). This sin could not be allowed to mar the picture of the church before the world and allowing this to happen was a problem for Paul and drew an extremely strong reprimand from the Apostle.

After his strong rebuke about the corporate sin of allowing this sin to run rampant within the church, the Apostle tells the Corinthian church in 2 Corinthians 2:1–4 exactly where his heart was regarding their sin. Regarding his first letter to them Paul said, "For I *wrote to you out of much affliction and anguish of heart and with many tears*, not to cause you pain but to let you know the abundant love that I have for you" (2 Cor 2:4). Paul's heart was broken over their sinfulness and need for repentance. Sin's prevalence in the world should come as no surprise to us. However, the level of sin within the lives of those who claim the name of Christ and within the church today should rightly shock and dismay us. While we are all aware that we are not able to achieve perfection in this life we should be broken over the sinfulness of God's people that, sometimes, seems to be practiced openly and ignored because we are afraid, we may lose offerings, or our attendance may dip. May we be rightly broken over the sinfulness of God's people, ourselves included, and call everyone to repentance.

It should also be noted that the Apostle Paul gives us insight as to *why* he wrote them through anguish of heart and many tears. While we must boldly call Christ's church to purity and holiness, we should never be motivated out of a sense of self-righteousness but, instead, from the same principle motivating Paul. Paul's bold and forthright call to repentance rose from his deep love for the Corinthian believers and his desire to see them restored in holiness. We can never back down from the calling to identify sin for what it is and clearly declare the truth of the Word of God and the need for holiness among His people. However, even Paul's rebuke came from a place of brokenness over their sin, his love for them, and a desire to see them come to repentance. We must have a deep love for Christ's bride, the church, and a deep desire to see her presented to Christ, "in splendor, without spot or wrinkle or any such thing, that she might be holy and without blemish" (Eph 5:27). When we are overwhelmed with this desire then we will be rightly broken over our own sin and sin among the people of God.

Broken Over False Teaching

The issue of false teaching within the church was of paramount importance to the Apostle Paul as can be seen in his letters to his young ministry apprentices, Timothy and Titus. In all three of these pastoral letters Paul instructs and warns these pastors against those who would inevitably arise and convince people regarding things that are not according to sound teaching.[6] Paul first visited Philippi during his second missionary journey and established the church there, which is recorded in Acts 16:11–40. After establishing the church in Philippi, the Apostle Paul wrote a letter to the Philippians to both instruct and encourage them. However, during this letter of encouragement, the Apostle instructed the Philippian believers to

---

6. 1 Tim 1:3–7, 19–20; 4:1–2; 6:3–5; 2 Tim 2:16–18; 3:1–8; 3:12–14; 4:2–5; Titus 1:11, 13–14.

imitate him as he walked with Christ because they needed to guard themselves against something or, rather, someone. Paul tells the Philippians they need to keep focused on walking in righteousness, "For many, of whom *I have often told you and now tell you even with tears*, walk as enemies of the cross of Christ" (Phil 3:18). The Apostle Paul is brought to a place of brokenness and tears over the false teaching/living of those who walk among them, even in the church.

Paul's brokenness over false teaching and the possibility of its leading believers astray should be seen as a clarion call today. False teaching is insidious and finds its way into our churches all too easily, whether it's through popular curriculum, the lyrics of a popular song, the words of a popular book, a popular conference speaker or heaven forbid, within the pulpit itself. As we understand the danger of false teaching, we should become ever more vigilant as we look to convey the truth of the message of Jesus Christ and, as we lead the people of God, we must be broken over false teaching and desire for our people, like Paul:

> That [their] love may abound more and more, with knowledge and all discernment, so that [they] may approve what is excellent, and so be pure and blameless for the day of Christ, filled with the fruit of righteousness that come through Jesus Christ, to the glory and praise of God (Phil 1:9–11).

Anticipate Opposition in Ministry

While it may be true that some ministry situations are attended by more difficult circumstances and details, all gospel ministry will experience opposition and those who seek to fulfill this ministry will experience difficulty as well. All too often there are those who enter the ministry believing that, by virtue of their calling, they will be loved by all. Then, as they enter ministry in the local church, they are surprised to find that not everyone agrees with them, not everyone has the same goals, not everyone likes them. In his letter to the young pastor Timothy, the Apostle Paul describes the difficulty and persecution he experienced during his missionary journeys and how the Lord delivered him. Then, in a wonderful promise to all believers and, for our purposes, all of us who are called to minister the gospel, "Indeed, all who desire to live a godly life in Christ Jesus will be persecuted . . . " (2 Tim 3:12). Living for Christ and, by Paul's example, pursuing the gospel ministry, will certainly be accompanied by mistreatment from those who will oppose or seek to hinder the work of God and the advance of the kingdom. Now we are not necessarily being persecuted just because someone disagrees with our leadership decisions; however, when we make a stand on the truth of God's Word and we are opposed, we are maligned, we are persecuted, and we should not be surprised. In the gospel ministry there are certainly high moments when people hear the gospel message, or right doctrine, and accept them in immense joy and, in these moments, we should celebrate. There will also be those who withstand the gospel, right doctrine, and the leading of the Holy Spirit and we must never run from the trial in fear. The trials are not something we will enjoy but they must certainly be something we anticipate in ministry.

> 1 Peter 4:12–14 "Beloved, do not be surprised at the fiery trial when it comes upon you to test you, as though something strange were happening to you. But rejoice insofar as you share Christ's sufferings, that you may also rejoice and be glad when His glory is revealed. If you are insulted for the name of Christ, you are blessed, because the Spirit of glory and of God rests upon you."

> Prayer Point: Lord, forgive *me* where *I* have become calloused toward people, please keep *me* from this. God, cultivate within *me* a heart that is broken for the lost, a heart broken over sin, and a heart that is broken over false teaching. Lord, give *me* the strength to never back down in the face of opposition to the gospel so that You may receive all the glory. Father, make *me* ready to minister with compassion, boldness, and wisdom for Your name's sake. Amen.

Chapter 4

A Bold Ministry

"And David said to Saul, 'Let no man's heart fail because of him. Your servant will go and fight with this Philistine.'"
— DAVID, SON OF JESSE (1 SAM 17:32) —

Acts 20:18b-20 "You yourselves know how I lived among you the whole time from the first day that I set foot in Asia, serving the Lord with all humility and with tears and with trials that happened to me through the plots of the Jews; how *I did not shrink back* from declaring to you anything that was profitable, and *teaching you in public* and from house to house,"

Commentary

Among the numerous objectives the Apostle Paul achieves in his farewell address to the Ephesian elders in Acts 20 is the task of reminding them of the *boldness* of his ministry. Paul's boldness in ministry not only served to honor the Lord whom he represented, but also set an example for all elders afterward. So then, Paul appeals to his own example of boldness in order to defend his integrity and to put forward for the Ephesian elders, and all ministers who follow, a premier example of *bold ministry*.

In Acts 20:19b, the Apostle calls the Ephesian elders as witnesses to the integrity of his ministry, saying, "You yourselves know . . . ". Here, the Ephesian elders are exhorted to recall Paul's living example. These

Ephesians were *physically present* to witness the entirety of Paul's ministry in Asia. These eyewitnesses could confirm the validity of Paul's ministerial practices. In verse 19, the Apostle calls them to remember that the marks of his legitimate ministry included: humility, sincerity, empathy (his "tears"), and suffering (his "trials"). Amid great suffering and persecution, the "plots of the Jews," Paul did not succumb to the pressure, nor did he shirk his responsibility as the Apostle of Christ, nor did he alter the message to assuage his opponents. Rather than being an unfaithful coward, Paul refused to "shrink from declaring" and made no attempt to hide. Instead, he taught in "public and from house to house, testifying to both Jews and to Greeks of repentance toward God and of faith in our Lord Jesus Christ" (vv. 20–21).

The Apostle's faithfulness to Christ was especially marked by boldness. In verse 20, Paul emphasizes his own boldness by refuting an accusation of the shameful sin of ministerial cowardice, saying, "I did not shrink back." Here, Paul negates the verb, "*hypesteilamēn*," which describes the practice of *holding oneself back from doing something*, even conveying (by way of implication) a fearful concern. In the face of danger or opposition, men are always tempted to be timid and cower, a cowardice that has lured many to turn their back on the offense of the gospel and embrace a message the world desires and the Lord Jesus despises.

Recall Paul's instruction to the young pastor Timothy, especially as it relates to the temptation *to shrink back* in cowardice in the face of opposition or persecution. There in 2 Timothy 1:7, the Apostle told his disciple, "For God gave us a spirit not of fear [*deilias*] but of power and love and self-control." In that portion of Scripture, one only needs to read the next two verses to see what would possibly tempt Timothy to have a fearful spirit and *shrink back*: "Therefore do not be ashamed of the testimony about our Lord, nor of me His prisoner, but share in suffering for the gospel by the power of God" (2 Tim 1:8). There is no question that Paul had experienced the temptation *to shrink back* and *be ashamed* in the face of suffering, and he certainly had many opportunities to give in to that temptation! However, just as he told the Ephesians elders, he refused *to shrink back* due to the threat of suffering and determined, rather, to be bold in his ministry.

> Ministry Principle: Boldness, for the minister, is not always natural and he should never take it for granted. There may be temptations to lack boldness but because the indwelling presence of the Holy Spirit within the minister there is never a good excuse for cowardice. What we need in a day of fear is *a bold ministry*.

A Bold Ministry

A Portrait of a Bold Ministry

Long is the list of faithful men of God who carried out bold ministry, but no list would be complete without mention of Martin Luther. When John Tetzel came into Germany to preach the false doctrines of the Catholic church, including the doctrines of purgatory and indulgences, Martin Luther was infuriated with righteous indignation. In response, Luther nailed his *Ninety-Five Theses* to the door of the castle church in Wittenberg, Germany, condemning these false doctrines and demanding the reformation of the church. Luther went on to publish the *Ninety-Five Theses* in German for the common man and sent a copy directly to Prince Albert. Deemed by the Catholic church a heretic and a divisive man, Luther remained undeterred in his course, despite the calls for his torment and execution. In Luther's time, wolves led the church! They preyed on people whom they had rendered ignorant by depriving them of the Word of God, they robbed them financially, they gave them false hope through false teaching, and most egregiously, they deprived them of the biblical gospel. Pope Leo wrongly declared Martin Luther to be a boar in the Lord's vineyard, because Luther was truly a shepherd fiercely guarding the people of God by fighting off the wolves in papal clothing. Surely Luther was tempted with cowardice and timidity, but the Lord upheld him and used him as His courageous and bold instrument to rediscover the biblical gospel for His church.

Oft persecuted for their obedience to Christ, the Apostles knew very well the temptation of ministerial cowardice and timidity. Recall the ministry of Peter and the other Apostles in the early chapters of Acts. There, we read that "many signs and wonders were regularly done among the people by the hands of the Apostles" (Acts 5:12). As a result, the crowds flocked to the obedient Apostles, but there were those with the Apostles who were fearful and remained hidden, as Luke records, "None of the rest dared join them" (Acts 5:13). Jealous of the large following and growing esteem of the Apostles, the high priest rose with others and imprisoned Peter and the Apostles serving with him. You remember the account well, as that night the angel of the Lord freed them from the prison and commanded them to go back into the temple and proclaim Christ (Acts 5:17–21). When the high priest found that they had escaped from prison and were again preaching Christ publicly, the Apostles were brought before him and the Sanhedrin (the same legal body which put Christ forward for crucifixion!). Seeking to silence the Apostles, the high priest forbade them from preaching in the name of Jesus. During that moment, when Peter and the Apostles could have shrunk back in fear, anticipating the same fate of crucifixion which their Lord had endured, they were instead filled with all boldness! Peter and the Apostles responded decisively to their opponents, "We must obey God rather than men" (Acts 5:29).

The boldness that Peter and the Apostles demonstrated that day is the kind of boldness we need in our ministers today. Paul Washer once said, "I've come to believe that being a coward runs in the blood of every man I've ever met, including myself. We must fight being cowards. And we must fight self-preservation. Christians are supposed to suffer. Pastors are supposed to suffer. It's what we do. And if by taking the truth of the gospel, we lose our positions, we lose our places, then so be it. At least we've been faithful to Him."[1]

So then, how do we overcome the temptation to *cowardice*, or as Paul wrote, the temptation "to shrink back"? I am convinced that there are four keys to being bold in the service of the Lord Jesus, and that is exactly what Jesus demands and what we need: a bold ministry. In order to have a bold ministry, you must be regenerate, faithful, hopeful, and fearful.

How to Have Boldness: You Must Be Born Again

How sad that a paragraph with this title needs to be written. The fact is, without the indwelling presence of the Holy Spirit, a pastor does not have the moral capacity to be boldly obedient for Christ. A man who occupies the office of pastor who is not born again is not only unqualified to be a pastor; he has not even met the qualifications to enter the kingdom of God (John 3:5–7).

To be born again (regenerate) is to have a new nature; it is to be a new creation in Christ Jesus (2 Cor 5:17), created by the powerful working of God through His Holy Spirit. This is what Jesus meant when He said, "Everyone who is born of the Spirit" (John 3:8). In the new birth, God grants to us not only all the promises of salvation and eternal inheritance, but as a down payment and guarantee of that inheritance, He places His Holy Spirit within us (Eph 1:13–14).

Take note then, as we looked previously at Paul's admonition to Timothy, "For God gave us a spirit [*pneuma*] not of fear but of power and love and self-control" (2 Tim 1:7). The "*pneuma*" (Spirit) Paul wrote of in this verse is the Holy Spirit. God's Spirit, which he gave us, is not a spirit of

---

1. Washer, "How to Reform a Church," 00:37.

cowardice and fear, but of power and love and self-control! So then, in order to have the boldness required for ministry, you must be indwelt by the Holy Spirit—you must be born again!

How to Have Boldness: You Must Be Faithful

I am convinced that the most accessible path to boldness in ministry is to firmly understand that you are called to be faithful. You are not responsible for *the outcome* of your ministry (the fruitfulness), as it is God who gives growth (1 Cor 3:6). You are, however, responsible to be faithful to the calling of the Lord Jesus and the Word that He has commanded you to proclaim. The Apostle Paul's command to Timothy is just as applicable to ministers today, "Fulfill your ministry" (2 Tim 4:5).

No matter the outcome, our responsibility is to be found faithful by our Lord, "Moreover, it is required of stewards that they be found faithful" (1 Cor 4:2). We are tempted to embrace cowardice when there is a price to pay for preaching hard biblical truths or for applying biblical truth in difficult circumstances in the life of the local church. In those times, your place as a minister in that congregation may be at risk, you may endure consequences or circumstances that are heavy and hard to bear. You may be tempted to avoid those consequences by being a coward, but you must remember to be found faithful to the only One whose judgment matters; remembering that His judgment is eternal! Let us consider the testimony of the Apostle Paul, who endured much suffering in his faithful service to the Master:

> And now, behold, I am going to Jerusalem, constrained by the Spirit, not knowing what will happen to me there, except that the Holy Spirit testifies to me in every city that imprisonment and afflictions await me. But I do not account my life of any value nor as precious to myself, if only I may finish my course and the ministry that I received from the Lord Jesus, to testify to the gospel of the grace of God (Acts 20:22-24).

How to Have Boldness: You Must Be Hopeful

To be bold in ministry, you must be hopeful. You must be hopeful of God's help as you minister in trying times. You must engage those difficult conversations as you apply biblical truth in the life of the church. You do this with the hope that "God may perhaps grant them repentance leading to a knowledge of the truth" (2 Tim 2:24).

To be bold in ministry, you must be hopeful of God's faithfulness to fulfill His promises. Above all, we strive as followers of Jesus to receive that glorious judgment, "Well done, good and faithful servant. You have been faithful over a little; I will set you over much. Enter into the joy of your master" (Matt 25:23). Hope sets your eyes on the reward, not the suffering which must be endured on the path to the reward. Of Jesus, the writer of Hebrews directs us to look to Jesus, "the founder and perfecter of our faith, who for the joy that was set before Him endured the cross, despising the shame, and is seated at the right hand of the throne of God" (Heb 12:2). In the same way Jesus set His hope on the joy that was before Him and endured suffering, so we set our hope on the reward that Christ has set before us as we serve Him. Let us once more be reminded of the example set for us by the Apostle Paul, "As it is my eager expectation and hope that I will not at all be ashamed, but that with full courage now as always Christ will be honored in my body, whether by life or by death. For to me to live is Christ, and to die is gain" (Phil 1:20–21).

How to Have Boldness: You Must Be Fearful

To be bold in ministry, you must be fearful (paradoxical to be certain). While fear can be a motivator toward cowardice, fear can also be a powerful catalyst to boldness. We can all be tempted at times to succumb to the fear of man, but the key to overcoming the fear of man is to embrace the fear of God. Jesus said, "And do not fear those who kill the body but cannot kill the soul. Rather fear Him who can destroy both soul and body in hell" (Matt 10:28).

To fear man is to be caught in a trap, but to fear the Lord is to be delivered from that trap, just as we read in Proverbs 29:25, "The fear of man lays a snare, but whoever trusts in the Lord is safe." Whoever you fear, you obey. None of us enjoy the hatred or ridicule of man, but the judgments of men are temporary. Only the judgment of God endures throughout all eternity. So then, to have a bold ministry, you must embrace the fear of the Lord. Do what is right, no matter what, and honor the Lord because you know you will give an account to Him. "So, whether we are at home or away, we make it our aim to please Him. For we must all appear before the judgment seat

A Bold Ministry

of Christ, so that each one may receive what is due for what he has done in the body, whether good or evil" (2 Cor 5:9–10).

Proverbs 28:1 "The wicked flee when no one pursues, but the righteous are bold as a lion."

Prayer Point: Lord, may *I* be bold in *my* obedience to You as *my* Master. You have so graciously and powerfully made *me* a brand-new creation in Christ Jesus. You have also entrusted *me* with this high-calling ministry. While I am tempted at times to fear man, may it be that You make *me* faithful to fulfill the ministry You have entrusted to *me*. May You fill *me* through Your Word with awareness of the promises You have made for those who love and obey You, so that *I* may set *my* hope on them. Lord, will you help *me* to never fall into the snare of fearing man, but keep *my* eyes and fear set on You, knowing that I will give an account to You for what *I* have done in this body.

Chapter 5

A Gospel-centered Ministry

"The gospel is only good news if it gets there in time."
— CARL F. H. HENRY[1] —

Acts 20:21 "... testifying both to Jews and to Greeks of *repentance toward God* and of *faith in our Lord Jesus Christ.*"

Commentary

Paul set out not to defend his ministry but encouraged the Ephesian elders to follow his ministry example. Paul was fearless in his gospel proclamation – in his "testifying." The word *testifying* (*diamartyromenos*) also occurs in verse 23 as *warns* and again in verse 24 as *testify*. This fearless message culminates in his faithful declaration of the *whole counsel of God* (v. 27). Typical of Paul's ministry was the inclusive nature of his *testifying*. He preached to all, both Jew and Gentile (Greeks), "This continued for two years, so that all the residents of Asia heard the word of the Lord, both Jews and Greeks" (Acts 19:10).

Indeed, Paul was the Apostle to the Gentiles, but he never forgot the synagogue. While Paul's audience may have been inclusive – *to all peoples*, the nature of his message was exclusive – *salvation is available only in Jesus* (Acts 4:12). His preaching focused on *repentance toward God* and *faith in*

---

1. Quoted in Thornbury, *Recovering Classic Evangelicalism*, 175.

our Lord Jesus – a subject unique for salvation. His message was both poignant and pointed – *turn from one's life of sin and place one's trust in Jesus*. "Repentance toward God, and faith in our Lord Jesus Christ" is about as compact and concise a way as we could have of summarizing Christian conversion . . . It is the gospel reduced to its simplest terms."[2] Paul's message and ministry was truly centered around the gospel of the Lord Jesus.

> Ministry Principle: ministry can be many things to many people, but what we need is a ministry based on and grounded in the Lord Jesus Christ, therefore a *gospel-centered ministry*.[3] This is not just theory but also practice.

A Portrait of a Gospel-centered Ministry

I (Tony) began listening to Dr. John MacArthur in my late teens. He has pastored Grace Community Church for over 50 years and is a stalwart verse-by-verse expositor of God's Word, who employs an undergirding historical and grammatical hermeneutic. On June 5, 2011, Dr. MacArthur completed a remarkable feat as he finished his 42-year journey of preaching through the New Testament verse-by-verse. To say his preaching has influenced me would be a significant understatement. There are more volumes in my library penned by him than any other author. An analysis of his preaching is an integral part of my doctoral dissertation. MacArthur is no stranger to controversy but, in general, any such storm is related to his understanding and defense of the gospel.[4] While some may view him as

---

2. Phillips, *Exploring Acts*, 402.

3. There are numerous articulations of this theological perspective. Many prefer "Gospel-centered" language (*gospel-centered, gospel-focused, gospel-shaped*) as opposed to "Christ-centered" language (*Christ-centered, Christ-focused, Christ-shaped*). For a "Gospel-centered" focus see Carson and Keller, *Gospel-Centered Ministry*, 1. For a "Christ-centered" defense see Kocman, "Be Christ-Centered, Not Just Gospel-Centered," Founders Ministries, March 18, 2019. For a balanced position see Challies, "The Gospel-Centered Everything," Challies.com, March 7, 2013. The authors make no distinction between "Christ-centered" and "Gospel-centered" (or for that matter "Cross-centered" language). To be "Gospel-centered" is to be "Christ-centered" and vice-versa. The point is Christ, and His gospel are front and center in all the minister *is* and *does*.

4. MacArthur even states, "I do not enjoy controversy. I realize I am sometimes cast in the role of controversialist, but the only times I have willingly entered into public controversy have been when I have perceived some teaching as a threat to biblical authority or the purity of the gospel." MacArthur, *Gospel According to Jesus*, 282.

"standing against *many* things," they would in fact be incorrect, for instead, he actually "stands for" *one* thing – the gospel. Whatever subverts the gospel, John MacArthur is faithful and gracious in opposing.

His first sermon at Grace reflects this – *How to Play Church* (Matt 7:21–23):

> Not everyone who says to me, 'Lord, Lord,' will enter the kingdom of heaven, but the one who does the will of my Father who is in heaven. On that day many will say to me, 'Lord, Lord, did we not prophesy in your name, and cast out demons in your name, and do many mighty works in your name?' And then will I declare to them, 'I never knew you; depart from me, you workers of lawlessness.'

His preaching and ministry reflect that passage – for many that say they believe the gospel still do not know the Lord, no matter how religious. Of all MacArthur's many publications, it is obvious he has a passion for the gospel – its proper definition, its proper presentation, and how one biblically reflects it against other so-called pseudo-gospels that so insidiously creep into the church. Not meant to be exhaustive, MacArthur has defended the gospel against the Charismatic and Prosperity movements, the Seeker Sensitive Movement, Roman Catholicism, Psychology and Psychiatry devoid of any biblical basis, Social Justice based on a blurred worldview, and non-Lordship Salvation. Reflecting on some titles and books with "gospel" emphasis:

- *Ashamed of the Gospel* – the gospel vs. pragmatism and the Seeker Sensitive movement
- *The Gospel According to God* – study of the "Old Testament's gospel" – Isaiah 53
- *The Gospel According to Paul* – review of the gospel based on the writings of Paul
- *The Gospel According to Jesus* – the gospel and the debate over "lordship salvation"
- *The Gospel According to the Apostles* – Paul and James, cheap grace, works
- *Good News: the Gospel of Jesus Christ* – Jesus asks: "who do you say that I am?"
- *On "Social Justice" and the Gospel* – the gospel vs. social justice

A Gospel-centered Ministry

- *The Vanishing Conscience and Hard to Believe* – culture-driven perceptions of moral accountability and the demands of the gospel.
- *The Jesus You Can't Ignore* – how to deal with false teachers and false gospels
- *Strange Fire* – the gospel vs. false teaching of the Charismatic/Prosperity movement
- *Nothing but the Truth* – communicate the truth of the gospel—with the right attitude
- *Only Jesus* – What does the gospel mean when it says to follow Jesus?

Dr. MacArthur typifies the gospel-centered ministry we need. His theology, ministry, and preaching reflect both a *passion for* and a *protectiveness of* the gospel. Much like Paul, a gospel-centered ministry will face opposition, "But though we had already suffered and been shamefully treated at Philippi, as you know, we had boldness in our God to declare to you the *gospel of God* in the midst of much conflict." (1 Thess 2:2). A reminder to us all:

> The gospel itself is disagreeable, unattractive, repulsive, and alarming to the world. It exposes sin, condemns pride, convicts the unbelieving heart, and shows human righteousness – even the best, most appealing aspects of human nature – to be worthless, filthy rags (cf. Isa. 64:6). It affirms that the real problems in life are not because of anyone but ourselves. We are fallen sinners, with deceitful hearts, evil motives, pervasive pride . . . It comes as bad news to those who love sin, and many who hear it for the first time react with disdain against the messenger.[5]

As I am writing, Dr. MacArthur is making a stand for religious liberty and the defense of the gospel against political forces in California involving governmental gathering mandates per COVID-19. You do not have to agree with his stance but alas, all you hear are crickets as many evangelical leaders remain silent as he stands against Caesar. While others choose to sing *kumbaya* and hold hands with the world, MacArthur instead chooses to earnestly "contend for the faith that was delivered to the saints once for all" (Jude 1:3). It seems he is always "out in front" making a stand for the gospel. Jon Benzinger speaks to the fact that some believe they will stand when it matters:

---

5. MacArthur, *Truth Matters*, 102–103.

No, they won't! This is wishful thinking at best and self-delusion at worst for one overwhelming reason: John MacArthur can do what he's doing because he has convictions. Oh, people will have convictions—don't get me wrong—but instead of coming from the truth (John 17:17), they will come uncritically from their upbringing, a hierarchy they trust, heroes they admire, or the cultural overlords who are all too ready to choose their convictions for them . . . In the end, you may not agree with John MacArthur, but he doesn't care, and neither should you. What you should be asking about John MacArthur is not, "Do I agree with what he's doing?" Instead ask, "Will I have his courage when it's my turn to stand?"[6]

Defining the Gospel

Since the ministry we need is a *gospel-centered* ministry we must answer an initial question. "What is the gospel?" Paul explained the gospel:

> Now I would remind you, brothers, of *the gospel* I preached to you, which you received, in which you stand . . . For I delivered to you as of first importance what I also received: *that* Christ died for our sins in accordance with the Scriptures, *that* he was buried, *that* he was raised on the third day in accordance with the Scriptures" (1 Cor 15:1, 3–4).

He goes on to say that Peter, all the Apostles, James and over 500 believers eye-witnessed this gospel as a historically accurate occurrence.

There is no redefining what God has defined; our ministry and message must be "Christ-focused and gospel-centered."[7] That being said, ministers and churches must heed Timothy Keller's advice, "It is one thing to have a ministry that is *gospel believing* and even *gospel proclaiming* but quite another to have one that is *gospel centered*."[8] But how does a pastor minister in a "gospel-centered" way? To be "gospel-centered" he will do so in what he *believes*, in what he *does*, and in what he *proclaims*.

---

6. Benzinger, "Courageous Example of John Macarthur," para. 11, 13.
7. Wax, *Gospel-Centered Teaching*, 25.
8. Keller, *Center Church*, 21.

A Gospel-centered Ministry

Gospel-centered in What He Believes – Theology

Before we define proper ministry practice, it is essential to understand what constitutes proper belief relating to *gospel-centeredness*. Since it is a ministry that focuses on Christ and the gospel, then His supernatural birth, sinless nature and life, substitutionary death and life-giving resurrection should serve as the wellspring of all the minister's thinking. For the glory of God, the pastor labors to make his theology of the person and work of Christ the driving force of all that he does, but it also provides the impetus of all other biblical doctrine and practice.

The minister understands that this principal verse alone elicits thoughts on what one believes about the doctrines pertaining to God, Christ, man, sin, and salvation. Paul's call for repentance and faith based on this "good news" and "*repentance toward God and of faith in our Lord Jesus Christ*" supply an inextricable link between repentance and faith. To possess faith is to repent; without repentance faith is impossible.[9] Wayne Gruden points out that, "Genuine repentance involves a deep sense that the worst thing about one's sin is that is has offended a holy God."[10] This is more than simple regret or sorrow.

The minister recognizes that *gospel-centeredness* views the Old Testament as pointing to and teaching in seed form what the New Testament fully unveils. The overarching theme of the inspired Scriptures then is God's redemptive work in Christ and His glorification. This *gospel-centeredness* is the bedrock of Christian doctrine. It is not just the way of explaining the doctrine of redemption, it is the heart of biblical teaching and should be at the heart of what the man of God believes.[11] It is this view that brings life to all who believe it and lifelessness to all who fail to do so, "You search the Scriptures because you think that in them you have eternal life; and it is *they that bear witness about me*, yet you refuse to come to me that you may have life" (John 5:39–40). You may be Christian, and even a Christian

---

9. Enns, *Moody Handbook of Theology*, 99–100.

10. Grudem, *Bible Doctrine*, 310.

11. Not long ago I heard of a conversation between ministers during the COVID pandemic. One stated, "I know the preaching of the gospel is important, *but* sometimes we also need to remember that checking on our staff during this time is just as important." Have we forgotten the admonition of Paul concerning the gospel, "For I delivered to you *as of first importance* what I also received" (1 Cor 15:3)? When someone introduces a comparative conjunction (*but*) to the gospel equation it reveals a dramatic lack of gospel-centeredness.

minister, but do your beliefs represent a hodgepodge of ideas, people and narratives from an ancient book or an understanding that there is a scarlet thread of redemption from the first word to the last that is still speaking today?

Gospel-centered in What He Does – Ministry

Those of us who would concur with the premise that orthodoxy leads to orthopraxy must be careful to remember that God defines both. Churches and ministries litter the ecclesiastical landscape deemed successful in their praxis – for they are successful to the degree that God says they are successful! "For you say, I am rich, I have prospered, and I need nothing, not realizing that you are wretched, pitiable, poor, blind, and naked" (Rev 3:17). The gospel-centered pastor does not put his hope in ministry practices, passing fads, the wisdom of this world's devices or whatever the ministerial flavor of the month offers. He grounds his convictions and practice in the Word of God.

Faced with an endless litany of issues from his members, hostility, and disapproval from without and within, he must be tenacious to be *gospel-centered*, ministering Christ to every person and circumstance. *Gospel-centeredness* is the heart of his work, and his ministry fleshes out "be strengthened by the grace that is in Christ Jesus" (2 Tim 2:1). It makes no difference if it is preaching, teaching, evangelism, discipleship, counseling, or leadership, the *gospel-centered* pastor brings to bear the power and sufficiency of the Word and the gospel in every arena.

I am a child of the conservative resurgence of the SBC. On more than one occasion I have had both professor and pastor utter words like this – "We have won the battle for the Bible at least in terms of inerrancy, but it is not over; the next great battle will be over the sufficiency of Scripture." These men were prophetic, or at least observant; it is unfolding before our eyes – a mindset that the Bible is not enough, it needs help. Worldly strategies and fashionable trends that are more in line with Hollywood than Holy Writ, with *cultural mores* more than Christian doctrine, worldly wisdom that Paul condemned in 1 Corinthians 1–2. Why should or would today's pastor buy what the world is selling, when he already owns what Christ secured? The gospel-centered pastor understands that in *doing* ministry God did not leave him powerless against the *god of this world* and the forces of this age, He left him with the strongest force in the cosmos – the effectual power to conquer sin. How so? Because the gospel is *the power of God* for: 1) salvation, "For I am not ashamed of the gospel, for *it is the power of God for salvation* to everyone who believes, to the Jew first and also to the Greek" (Rom 1:16), 2) sanctification, "And by which you *are being* saved, if you hold fast to the word I preached to you—unless you believed in vain" (1 Cor 15:2), and 3) mission, "Go therefore and *make disciples* of all nations, baptizing them in the name of the Father and of the Son and of the Holy Spirit, teaching them to observe all that I have commanded you. And behold, I am with you always, to the end of the age" (Matt 28:19–20).

As earlier stated, one may believe the gospel and still not have a *gospel-centered* ministry. There are some who insist that is what they have, but they tragically cry out for other pseudo-solutions that bit by bit poison their listeners instead of providing remedy. We must saturate everything we do with the gospel. A *gospel-centered* ministry is dissimilar to other ministry models. That is not to say that the world or, God forbid, even segments of His church will not applaud or imbibe, but that is not the point – the point is *"Is God pleased?"* The power of personality, shiny new toys, attractive programs, worldly means, incessant tweeting or posting about self or any other *non-gospel-centered* trifle and buffoonery is not the ministry we need, we need a *gospel-centered* ministry.

Gospel-centered in What He Proclaims – Preaching

The driving force of this chapter was Acts 20:21 " . . . testifying both to Jews and to Greeks of *repentance toward God and of faith in our Lord Jesus Christ."* In short, Paul proclaimed the gospel. Inspired by the Spirit, Paul stated this central biblical message of the gospel and his preaching in many dynamic ways: "For I decided to know nothing among you except *Jesus Christ and him crucified*" (1 Cor 2:2), "*Him we proclaim*, warning everyone and teaching everyone with all wisdom, that we may present everyone mature in Christ" (Col 1:28), "That is, *in Christ God was reconciling the world to himself*, not counting their trespasses against them, and entrusting to us the message of reconciliation" (2 Cor 5:19), and simply but powerfully "For I am not ashamed of *the gospel*, for it is the power of God for salvation to everyone who believes, to the Jew first and also to the Greek" (Rom 1:16). Are there many expressions of Paul's proclamation? Yes. Are they true to the central biblical message? Most certainly!

Trevin Wax asks, "The question is not, "*Do* you open your Bible and comment on it?" but "*How* do you open the Bible and comment on it."[12] If our interest is *gospel-centered* preaching, we might ask ourselves, "What is missing from our sermons?" Good thought, but the better, more insightful question might be "*Who* is missing from our sermons?" Paul shows us, "For what we proclaim is not ourselves, but *Jesus Christ as Lord*, with ourselves as your servants for Jesus's sake" (2 Cor 4:5). The ministry of preaching we need is *gospel-centered*, our calling is proclaiming *Jesus Christ as Lord*, all else is either irrelevant or secondary.[13] God called Paul and he reasoned "in order that I might preach him" (Gal 1:16) – preach who? Him who *is the gospel*, "the gospel that was preached by me" (Gal 1:11). Charles Haddon Spurgeon stated his distaste of *Christless* sermons or sermons that are not *gospel-centered*. Here are two samplings:

> The motto of all true servants of God must be, 'We preach Christ; and him crucified.' A sermon without Christ in it is like a loaf of bread without any flour in it. No Christ in your sermon, sir? Then go home, and never preach again until you have something worth preaching.[14]

> Leave Christ out? O my brethren, better leave the pulpit out altogether. If a man can preach one sermon without mentioning Christ's name in it, it ought to be his last, certainly the last that any Christian ought to go to hear him preach.[15]

Jerry Vines and Jim Shaddix state that, "Paul, in his beautiful and insightful summary of his ministry at Ephesus, defined his preaching content as "testifying . . . of repentance toward God, and of faith in our Lord Jesus Christ" (Acts 20:21).[16] R. Albert Mohler adds:

> Preaching is therefore always a matter of life and death . . . It is not enough to preach Christ without calling for belief and repentance. It is not enough to promise the blessings of heaven without warning of the threat of hell. It is not enough to preach salvation without pointing to judgment.[17]

---

12. Wax, *Gospel-Centered Teaching*, 78.
13. Olford and Olford, *Anointed Expository Preaching*, 14.
14. Spurgeon, "To You," 8.
15. Spurgeon, "Prayer for the Church Militant," 7.
16. Vines and Shaddix, *Power in the Pulpit*, 29.
17. Mohler, *He Is Not Silent*, 63, 130.

A Gospel-centered Ministry

Some opt for a Jesus not found in Scripture – a *non-gospel-centered* Jesus. Preaching Jesus without preaching Scripture or the whole of Scripture is to preach an *unknown* Jesus. Rob Gallaty and Steven Smith attest, "If Scripture is the means God chose to reveal Himself, then the message of Christ is only significant if it is tethered to the Scriptures."[18] How sad that many miss this mark today in their preaching. There is a possibility that we might preach a message based on biblical texts and still miss the fundamental message – we can preach the details without a sense of proclaiming how they relate to Christ.[19]

So how do we remain *gospel-centered* and *Christ-focused* in our preaching? Do we adhere to the clichéd Spurgeon admonition that no matter what you preach on, you make a *beeline to the cross*? Just a few quick insights: 1) Jesus Christ is neither a *postscript* nor an *attachment* to a message 2) preaching, *even gospel-centered, Christ-focused preaching* must have hermeneutical integrity and 3) the text must drive the message – *the text is the message*. Whatever the text preached is, the question is always the same – *Where does my text stand in relation to Christ*? Somehow there is connection in the text to the grand theme of Scripture – redemption in Christ. Many avenues suggest how one may arrive at a true *gospel-centered, Christ-focused*, hermeneutically sound proclamation: 1) *Christocentric* – Christ is the central theme of Scripture, 2) *Christotelic* – Christ is the ultimate end or goal of Scripture, or 3) *Christiconic* – the Bible as a whole projects images of Christ or His character as the goal in the lives of the readers (each text portrays a facet of what it looks like to be Christlike). Advocates of each propose their hermeneutic is appropriate to the demise of the others. Yet does it have to be either/or, or can it be both/and? Tony Merida explains, "Every text stands somewhere in relation to Christ. Every text will point to Christ futuristically, refer to Christ explicitly, or look back to Christ implicitly"[20]

Some preachers forget that the distinctive Christian feature about Christianity is *Christ*. So, *gospel-centered* preaching has Christ as the burning epicenter of its proclamation. Vines and Shaddix explain the ramifications of this distinctiveness in this way. For Christ is:

> The distinguishing factor between Christian preaching and the moralistic, God-themed sermons that characterize most theistic world religions ... [indeed] a truly Christian sermon should never

---

18. Gallaty and Smith, *Preaching for the Rest of Us*, 13.
19. Olford and Olford, *Anointed Expository Preaching*, 87.
20. Merida, *Faithful Preaching*, 41.

be welcome in a Jewish synagogue or a Muslim mosque, at least sermons spoken by preachers who have any convictions about what they believe.[21]

Jesus is not a character in the Bible, He is *the* character *of* the Bible. The pastor who preaches Christ and applies Christ in 10,000 ministry situations will realize what it means to be *gospel-centered*. Merida speaks about this notable goal:

> I believe that the redemptive purpose of Scripture (transforming people into Christ's image) is consistent with the redemptive message of Scripture. The Bible narrates the ongoing flow of redemptive history that moves ultimately to the person and work of Jesus. Therefore exposition, at its best, will move inexorably to Jesus as the hero of Scripture.[22]

So, if you preached in a Jewish synagogue, would it offend? If you preached in a Muslim mosque would people be upset with your Christ? When you do a wedding, or a funeral, is Christ even mentioned? Are you a preacher of the gospel or not?

> Proverbs 15:30 "The light of the eyes rejoices the heart, and *good news* refreshes the bones."

> Prayer Point: Lord, forgive *me* for my lack of gospel-centeredness in *my* theology, ministry, and proclamation. You have placed at *my* disposal the gospel – the power of God for salvation. Enable *me*, help *me* to remain focused and stay true to the "eternal gospel to proclaim to those who dwell on earth, to every nation and tribe and language and people" (Rev 14:6).

---

21. Vines and Shaddix, *Progress in the Pulpit*, 108.
22. Merida, *Faithful Preaching*, 40–41.

Chapter 6

A Spirit-led Ministry

*"The Spirit is the first power we experience,
but the last power we come to understand."*

— OSWALD CHAMBERS[1] —

Acts 20:22–23 "And now, behold, I am going to Jerusalem, *constrained by the Spirit*, not knowing what will happen to me there, except that *the Holy Spirit testifies to me* in every city that imprisonment and afflictions await me."

Commentary

Paul felt he *had* to go to Jerusalem, even though great trouble threatens that may take his life. The Spirit gave no sure word on his demise, but clearly Paul was willing to pay the price for the One who had redeemed him. His commitment to Christ surpassed any thought of self – this marked his life and ministry ever since Damascus. The Lord revealed to Ananias that Paul "must suffer for the sake of my name" (Acts 9:16) and the same Spirit that compelled him to Jerusalem is the same Spirit that warned him of impending suffering and imprisonment.[2]

---

1. Chambers, *Biblical Psychology*, 212.
2. A question for some is Luke's usage of *pneumati* in verse 22. Among oft used translations (CSB, NASB, ESV, NET, KJV) only the KJV renders it as *spirit* (i.e., the spirit

In every town he heard warning – some at Tyre warned him *through the Spirit* via prophetic inspiration, not to go to Jerusalem (Acts 21:4). He would not know the specifics until the Spirit prophesied through Agabus at Caesarea (Acts 21:11). Compelled to go *by the Spirit*, warned not to go *by the Spirit* – this would seem contradictory. Both compulsion and warning can be accurate – the message of the Spirit here is compatible, "Paul was indeed going to Jerusalem. God had a purpose for him going there. The warnings prepared him for what awaited him in Jerusalem and assured him that whatever happened, God was in it."[3]

Ministry Principle: *Spirit-led* conjures up all sorts of images, some biblical, some unbiblical. What we need is a ministry based not on experience or opinion but one fixed, dependent, and grounded on the revealed Holy Spirit of Scripture, therefore a *Spirit-led ministry*.

A Portrait of a Spirit-led Ministry

What does a Spirit-led ministry look like? Dr. Don Stephens became my (Tony) pastor when I was thirteen years old. Bro. Don was pastor to my family, as well as my wife and her family. That was 49 years ago. Even though I have been in ministry for over 40 years, I still consider him to be my pastor. He still pastors a church and still faithfully and powerfully preaches God's Word at the age of 85. As I write this, he is preparing to preach verse by verse through the book of Revelation to his flock.

Though he is not as active as he once was – the Holy Spirit's ministry, on him, in him and through him, has not diminished one scintilla over time. He has served the Lord as a seminary professor, revivalist, evangelist, and powerful personal witness, but views the office of pastor as his highest calling. He pastored in the once-called "pioneer missionary area" of North America and has done mission work in various mission posts around the world. He is expository preacher extraordinaire, master teacher, husband, father, grandfather, great grandfather, and mentor and in all these things – the Spirit consistently leads him.

---

of Paul, his determination, or resolve), all others translate it as *Spirit* (i.e., the indwelling Spirit led or compelled him). Each render these verses in close context as *pneuma* (20:23, 28; 21:11) or *pneumatos* (21:4) as *Spirit*; they render *pneumati* in 19:21 variously: *purposed in the Spirit* (NASB), *resolved by the Spirit* (CSB, ESV), *resolved* (NET), *decided* (NIV), *purposed in the spirit* (KJV). It seems best to see this as the indwelling *Spirit* compelling Paul's *spirit*.

3. Polhill, *NAC*, Acts, 425.

A Spirit-led Ministry

He would, no doubt, be upset that I am focusing on him instead of Jesus. Nevertheless, much like the Baptist of John's prologue, Bro. Don is:

> A man sent from God . . . He came as a witness, to bear witness about the light, that all might believe through him. He was not the light, but came to bear witness about the light. The true light, which gives light to everyone, was coming into the world" (John 1:6–9).

Like John, he reflects Someone greater, Someone he prefers to shine the light on – he is someone who allows the Holy Spirit to flow through him. Many times, the Spirit has mesmerized me as I have heard him tell the story of D. L. Moody's conversion and call:

> Moody's life illustrates the necessity of completely yielding to God. "The world has yet to see what God will do with and for and through and in and by the man who is fully and wholly consecrated to Him." "He said 'a man,'" thought Moody; "he did not say a great man, nor a learned man, nor a rich man, nor a wise man, nor an eloquent man, nor a 'smart' man, but simply 'a man.' I am a man, and it lies with the man himself whether he will or will not make that entire and full consecration. I will try my utmost to be that man.[4]

I suppose the reason the story sticks out in my memory – they are words about Moody, but they may as well be words about Bro. Don – he chose to be "that man." When you are around him, you sense his personal holiness and you realize it, as that holiness works itself out in vivid tangible ways. I grew up with words like unction, endowed, imbued, earnestness, fervor, zeal, passion, and empowerment. What of the preachers and preaching of our day? Greg Heisler is absolutely right, "The unfamiliarity many preachers have regarding the Spirit's power for preaching is lamentable."[5] We should be ashamed! Are those words I grew up with mere words or spiritual realities? Is our unfamiliarity with the Spirit due to our lack of personal and practical holiness and a preaching effort devoid of the Spirit?

A few notes about Bro. Don's preaching and the Spirit:

- He preached and there was one thing we all knew – the Spirit was going to move
- There was never manipulation in the movement – it was Spirit empowered

4. Moody, *Life of Dwight L. Moody*, 134.
5. Heisler, *Spirit-led Preaching*, 128.

- His preaching was and continues to be God-honoring, Christ-centered and Spirit-led
- There was never a time I thought – "That was a dud" or "That fell short"
- I have often thought – How can this be? There is only one answer – a man given over to the Spirit.

Many words come to mind when I think of Bro. Don – friend, encourager, mentor, teacher, pastor, motivator, challenger and to be sure, someone who is never frivolous about the things of God or the Spirit of God. I conclude with an incident when I was about 14. It was Thursday night visitation and I teamed up with Bro. Don. The large group prayed, and we separated to go on our assignments. As we closed the car doors, he looked over at me and said, "The people we are going to see tonight are lost and probably demon-possessed – if you are not right with God, my advice to you would be to get right before we get there because we do not know what awaits us." One of thousands of incidents that make up a Spirit-led ministry, "Not by might, nor by power, but by my Spirit, says the Lord of hosts" (Zech 4:6).

Defining the Work of the Spirit

The inimitable John Owen described the state of despising the person of the Holy Spirit and rejecting His work as equivalent to the Jews rejection of the person of the Son in the New Testament and the idolatry by Israel against God in the Old Testament.[6] While the true church will not plummet to those depths of rejection, sadly it seems that many in the church today have a skewed understanding of the Spirit. In many cases, the church seeks to avoid and ignore Him altogether or they are wandering dangerously close to the lunatic fringe. What we desperately need is understanding and balance.

To establish common biblical footing, a few definitions are in order. This is meant to be illustrative of the Spirit and not exhaustive. *Baptism of the Spirit* occurs simultaneously with salvation. It is the inward beginning work in the believer and happens only once. "For in one Spirit we were all baptized into one body—Jews or Greeks, slaves or free—and all were made to drink of one Spirit" (1 Cor 12:13). *Filling of the Spirit* is a continual inward

---

6. Owen, *Pneumatologia*, 26.

working of the Spirit in the life of the believer. "And do not get drunk with wine, for that is debauchery, but be filled with the Spirit" (Eph 5:18). The Luke/Acts narrative typifies this work of the Spirit. Individuals are said to be either *full of the Spirit* (Luke 4:1; Acts 6:3, 5; 7:55; 11:24) or *filled with the Spirit* (Luke 1:15, 41, 67; Acts 2:4; 4:8, 31; 5:3; 9:17; 13:52). Remarkably like this *filling* of the Spirit is the *anointing* of the Spirit. Some make no distinction between filling and anointing, but there seems to be a clear purpose for making the distinction.[7] *Anointing* is an inward working of the Spirit with an outward manifestation of power given especially in proclamation. "The Spirit of the Lord is upon me because he has anointed me to proclaim good news to the poor. He has sent me to proclaim liberty to the captives and recovering of sight to the blind, to set at liberty those who are oppressed" (Luke 4:18). One typically defines *illumination* as the understanding that the Holy Spirit enables believers whereby, they can grasp authorial intent and the meaning of the biblical text both intellectually and spiritually. In the area of proclamation, the above is true, but it also applies to the Spirit's enablement for the listener to understand and respond because he experiences *conviction*. Jerry Vines and Jim Shaddix state that "not only does the Holy Spirit illuminate our minds to truth. He also convicts those who hear it proclaimed . . . Conviction is the work of the Spirit in bringing people to the realization that God is right, and they are wrong."[8]

A Spirit-led heart – Personal Holiness

As we consider the areas of a Spirit-led ministry, none is as important as our personal walk with God. God promised the Spirit to believers and "we are witnesses to these things, and so is the Holy Spirit, *whom God has given to those who obey him*" (Acts 5:32). While this is true of all believers, it bears special significance for those who lead God's people – His ministers. Moses was ill-prepared to lead God's people until he recognized the holy nature of God's being. Donald Grey Barnhouse cogently points out that "the man who is to thunder in the court of Pharaoh with an imperious, "Thus saith the Lord!" must first stand barefoot before the burning bush."[9] There is

---

7. Jerry Vines and Jim Shaddix would favor this distinction, but are wise to conclude, "Anointing has close – if not synonymous – relationship with the idea of being filled with the Spirit." Vines and Shaddix, *Progress in the Pulpit*, 76.

8. Vines and Shaddix, *Progress in the Pulpit*, 73.

9. Barnhouse, "On Expository Preaching," 30.

an inextricable link between the man of God and personal holiness. The indwelling Holy Spirit creates an insatiable appetite for holiness as He not only seeks to magnify Christ but imparts a yearning within the man of God to be more like Christ.[10] Biblically speaking there is both an *already* and *not yet* reality pertaining to the Spirit. Already the believer is experiencing *positional holiness* (or positional sanctification). While the carnal Corinthian believers were unholy in many ways, still Paul addressed them as "to those *sanctified* in Christ Jesus, called to be *saints* [holy ones]" (1 Cor 1:2). He admonished believers in Colossae to add Christlike qualities to their character but addressed them as "God's chosen ones, *holy* and beloved" (Col 3:12)." As surely as their predestination and glorification are positionally secure, so is their holiness (Rom 8:29–20). As biblical as our holiness is positionally, it is just as biblical that there must be a practical "working it out" – *progressive holiness*. This process of becoming holy must be ongoing until we reach heaven and its realization. This is the emphasis of the New Testament – to be like Christ in holiness. God will do it, but it will involve an act of our will as Paul tells us, "To walk in a manner worthy of the calling to which you have been called" (Eph 4:1).

Paul paints a picture of life in the Spirit in Galatians 5 – here we see that the believer will either walk by the Spirit and produce His fruit and progress in holiness per verses 22–26:

> But the fruit of the Spirit is love, joy, peace, patience, kindness, goodness, faithfulness, gentleness, self-control; against such things there is no law. And those who belong to Christ Jesus have crucified the flesh with its passions and desires. If we live by the Spirit, let us also keep in step with the Spirit. Let us not become conceited, provoking one another, envying one another.

or they will walk in the flesh and progress in the deeds of darkness per verses 19–21:

> Now the works of the flesh are evident: sexual immorality, impurity, sensuality, idolatry, sorcery, enmity, strife, jealousy, fits of anger, rivalries, dissensions, divisions, envy, drunkenness, orgies, and things like these. I warn you, as I warned you before, that those who do such things will not inherit the kingdom of God.

The distinction becomes sharper when one considers that for those who walk in the deeds of darkness as a continuous practice, they "will not

---

10. Whitney, *Spiritual Disciplines*, 237.

inherit the kingdom of God." Bottom line, if you and I are not walking in the Spirit, then we are walking as the unregenerate. Gene Getz is correct when he writes, "The degree to which we live holy lives depends upon the extent to which we keep in step with the Holy Spirit and His plan for our lives.[11] Every Christian has a choice – walk *progressively* according to our *position* or walk in sin. Paul reminds us that "The night is far gone; the day is at hand. So then let us cast off the works of darkness and put on the armor of light . . . But put on the Lord Jesus Christ, and make no provision for the flesh, to gratify its desires" (Rom 13:12, 14). It behooves us as God's ministers to understand where we stand in relation to the Spirit. We can know we are in right standing "you who are spiritual" (Gal 6:1), then again, we can overestimate our progress, "For if anyone thinks he is something, when he is nothing, he deceives himself" (Gal 6:3).

How can we arrive at and thrive in a Spirit-led ministry? It can only come about through diligent attention to every area of sanctification, especially personal holiness.[12] This diligent attention is wrought by 1) the Spirit through His Word as we "Let the word of Christ dwell in you richly, teaching and admonishing one another in all wisdom" (Col 3:16), understanding "How can a young man keep his way pure? By guarding it according to your word" (Ps 119:9) and, 2) renewing our mind through Spirit and Word knowing that "whatever is true, whatever is honorable, whatever is just, whatever is pure, whatever is lovely, whatever is commendable, if there is any excellence, if there is anything worthy of praise, think about these things" (Phil 4:8) and "do not be conformed to this world, but be transformed by the renewal of your mind, that by testing you may discern what is the will of God, what is good and acceptable and perfect" (Rom 12:2). For a Spirit-led ministry we are pointing out three vital areas of personal holiness – moral purity, doctrinal purity, and devotional purity.[13]

Lack of personal holiness, especially concerning moral purity, is a deplorable thing for the man of God. *Leadership Magazine* interviewed 1,000 pastors – 12 percent had committed adultery while in ministry (1 out of 8) and 23 percent had done something they considered sexually

---

11. Getz, *Measure of a Man*, 229–230.

12. MacArthur, *Power of Integrity*, 125–126.

13. These 3 are non-negotiable. One would gravely err in limiting holiness to just these. Charles Spurgeon spoke of grieving the Spirit by such things as "want of sensitiveness (unfeeling from disobedience), want of truthfulness, scantiness of grace (absence spoils everything), pride, laziness, neglect of prayer." Spurgeon, *Lectures to My Students*, 212–213.

inappropriate.[14] John MacArthur states, "When believers or professing believers are immoral, the immediate consequences are especially bad, because the testimony of the gospel and all true Christians is damaged.[15] Sexual impurity is always sin and will always be judged and it makes no difference if it is personal, private or public. Hear the powerful warning from Paul:

> But sexual immorality and all impurity or covetousness must not even be named among you, as is proper among saints . . . For you may be sure of this, that everyone who is sexually immoral or impure, or who is covetous (that is, an idolater), has no inheritance in the kingdom of Christ and God. Let no one deceive you with empty words, for because of these things the wrath of God comes upon the sons of disobedience" (Eph 5:3, 5–6).

If there is any doubt about God's standard for holiness in the area of sexual purity, He forthrightly declares, "For this is the will of God, your sanctification: that you abstain from sexual immorality; that each one of you know how to control his own body in holiness and honor" (1 Thess 4:3–4).

To maintain holiness, there must be steadfastness or a standard of keeping pure in doctrine. If Satan can sidetrack us with unbiblical, questionable, and foolish doctrinal error, he will render us not only ineffective, but unholy. Paul was aghast that the Galatians had so quickly turned from the truth to imbibe in error:

> I am astonished that you are so quickly deserting him who called you in the grace of Christ and are turning to a different gospel—not that there is another one, but there are some who trouble you and want to distort the gospel of Christ. But even if we or an angel from heaven should preach to you a gospel contrary to the one we preached to you, let him be accursed (Gal 1:6–8).

The man of God must know better, but also do better and be better, "But as for you, O man of God, flee these things. Pursue righteousness, godliness, faith, love, steadfastness, gentleness" (1 Tim 6:11).

Finally, to be a Spirit-led minister with a heart devoted to personal holiness, the man of God must be a man of prayer. Being in constant contact with the Father will provide the means for devotional purity. Prayer is not simply a staunch belief, it is a fervent practice; it is at the forefront, not an afterthought. E. M. Bounds said it best many years ago:

---

14. Hughes, *Disciplines of a Godly Man*, 21–22.
15. MacArthur, *Power of Integrity*, 126.

> We are constantly on a stretch, if not on a strain, to devise new methods, plans, and organizations to advance the church and secure enlargement and efficiency for the gospel. This trend of the day has a tendency to lose sight of the man or sink the man in the plan or organization. God's plan is to make much of the man, far more of him than anything else. Men are God's method. The church is looking for better methods; God is looking for better men . . . What the church needs to-day is not more machinery or better, not new organizations or more and novel methods, but men whom the Holy Ghost can use -- men of prayer, men mighty in prayer. The Holy Ghost does not flow through methods, but through men. He does not come on machinery, but on men. He does not anoint plans, but men, men of prayer.[16]

How is your personal walk with the Lord – shoddy, non-existent or never enough? Do you go to the Word of God just for sermons or do you go to have an encounter with the King?

A Spirit-led walk – Practical Holiness

What would cause people to exercise extreme religious rituals such as flagellation or crawling up steps on their knees to the point of bleeding? They believe it somehow makes them approved by God and in some sense *holy*. They may be quite sincere, but they are sincerely misinformed and in error. Paul desired "that in every place the men should pray, lifting holy hands without anger or quarreling" (1 Tim 2:8) but certainly not those or any other ungodly means to obtain or maintain holiness. There are many perceived avenues one might pursue to obtain and maintain holiness: perfectionism (I can attain perfection in this life), asceticism (escape temptation by punishing their body), self-denial (become holy through the denial of what God has said is acceptable), or legalism (holiness through a set of rules). All these avenues to holiness are unacceptable because they are not God-ordained paths.

As we saw earlier, Spirit-led ministry finds its grounding in personal holiness. This personal holiness must flesh itself out into practical holiness in this world. Believers need not fear for "*I am sending the promise of my Father* upon you. But stay in the city until you are clothed with power from on high" (Luke 24:49). The whole matter of practical holiness is how we

---

16. Bounds, *Power through Prayer*, 11–12.

behave toward others. When we are walking by the Spirit (Gal 5:16) and allowing the Spirit to lead us (Gal 5:18) then it is a reality in this world and this leadership of the Spirit implies His lordship.[17] Romans 12:10–21 provides a great template for how our personal holiness practically relates to others:

> [How our practical holiness relates to other believers] Love one another with brotherly affection. Outdo one another in showing honor. Do not be slothful in zeal, be fervent in spirit, serve the Lord. Rejoice in hope, be patient in tribulation, be constant in prayer. Contribute to the needs of the saints and seek to show hospitality. [How our practical holiness relates to strangers] Bless those who persecute you; bless and do not curse them. Rejoice with those who rejoice, weep with those who weep. Live in harmony with one another. Do not be haughty, but associate with the lowly. Never be wise in your own sight. [How our practical holiness relates to our enemies] Repay no one evil for evil, but give thought to do what is honorable in the sight of all. If possible, so far as it depends on you, live peaceably with all. Beloved, never avenge yourselves, but leave it to the wrath of God, for it is written, "Vengeance is mine, I will repay, says the Lord." To the contrary, "if your enemy is hungry, feed him; if he is thirsty, give him something to drink; for by so doing you will heap burning coals on his head." Do not be overcome by evil, but overcome evil with good.

We find the clarion call of God's Word for Spirit-led ministry from God's mouth, "You shall be holy, for I the Lord your God am holy" (Lev 19:2). God never gives a command that He does not empower one with the ability to keep it – it is the classic imperative to *be holy*, grounded in the indicative *I, the Lord your God, am holy*. From the Old Testament we find Joseph, one who lived and modeled a holy life. Amazingly enough, Joseph accomplished this before the Law was ever given, before Jesus Christ ever modeled it, before the Holy Spirit ever indwelt or aided believers and before the Word of God was ever complete – how sad when ministers grieve and quench the Spirit, to what greater extent should we as Christians be able to live in holiness? We have *all* these resources at our disposal.[18] Some preachers may ask after ungodly behavior – Why did I do that? The answer is simple – a lack of practical holiness in the minister's life is due to his lack of personal holiness.

17. Olford and Olford, *Anointed Expository Preaching*, 37.
18. Getz, *Measure of a Man*, 232.

A Spirit-led proclamation – Anointed Preaching

The man of God who has a Spirit-led ministry, especially in his preaching, must by necessity depend on the Holy Spirit. This is true for numerous reasons, not the least – biblical comprehension. The Spirit no longer discloses new bits of revelation to him, but He will bring deeper awareness, understanding, and application of existing revelation (i.e. the Bible).[19] His dependence does not end there, for he knows that preparation is only part of the task, he must also deliver the message with accuracy and fervency for only the Spirit can transform a manuscript into a message.[20] The preacher, however, is only part of the equation. Anointed proclamation depends on the attending Spirit to illuminate not only the preacher, but his listeners as well, so the life-changing message of God's Word renders its transformative work.[21] Vines and Shaddix assert that anointed proclamation in a Spirit-led ministry is where:

> The preacher wants to know what the Spirit said when He inspired the biblical text, and he wants the Spirit to empower his communication when he preaches what the Spirit has said in the biblical text. That means we're in hot pursuit of the Holy Spirit's intended meaning in every text of Scripture, as well as His attending power to our proclamation of it . . . One thing, however, that you can't afford to ignore in your sermon preparation and presentation is your dependency on God's Holy Spirit.[22]

Having a Spirit-led ministry means experiencing *anointed* proclamation. The greatest example of this is Jesus Christ as he declares, "The Spirit of the Lord is upon me, because he has anointed me to proclaim good news to the poor. He has sent me to proclaim liberty to the captives and recovering of sight to the blind, to set at liberty those who are oppressed" (Luke 4:18). Here is Jesus, depending on the Spirit to redeem the bankrupt, release the bound, restore sight to the blind, relieve the burdened and the bruised. From Jesus's own words we see that *anointing* is associated with the task of proclamation or preaching. As stated earlier, anointing bears similarity to Spirit filling, the difficulty is in the explanation, still Spirit filling

---

19. Olford and Olford, *Anointed Expository Preaching*, 20.
20. Olford and Olford, *Anointed Expository Preaching*, 214.
21. Vines and Shaddix, *Progress in the Pulpit*, 71. R. Albert Mohler adds that "Both the preacher and the hearers are dependent upon the work of the Holy Spirit for any adequate understanding of the text." Mohler, *He Is Not Silent*, 45.
22. Vines and Shaddix, *Progress in the Pulpit*, 35, 388.

or anointing as a preacher differs from Spirit filling as a believer. Vines and Shaddix assert "Without a doubt, something mysterious is at play when the Holy Spirit attends to the preaching event. This fact can make any attempt to describe the work of the Spirit in the preaching very difficult."[23] It is as the old country preacher once said in trying to describe the mysterious inner workings of the Spirit in the preacher, "I may not know what it is, but I know what it ain't!" Arturo Azurdia explains anointed proclamation as "an *event*, a sovereign and spontaneous act of God related to the proclamation of truth . . . An instantaneous, sudden, and sovereign operation of the Spirit of God coming upon a man so that his proclamation of Jesus Christ might be attended by holy power."[24] So, *anointing* is for the purpose of the proclamation. Some prefer other terms such as unction, endowed, imbued, earnestness, fervor, zeal, passion or even empowerment.[25] Greg Heisler provides the characteristics of *anointing* or as he prefers *Spirit empowerment*, as freedom, vitality, power (unction), and possession in the preaching event.[26] If the purpose of anointing is for the proclamation of the preacher's message, then "how so?" Vines and Shaddix provide clarity:

> This ingredient enables the preachers' words to be pointed and powerful. This ingredient has been called the *anointing*. Some homileticians and preachers do not believe the anointing actually exists, contending it is an unnecessary and unbiblical notion that often weighs the preacher down with guilt. Scripture, however, seems to indicate there is some mysterious attendance of God's Spirit when His Word is proclaimed rightly . . . Spirit-anointed preaching does something to both preacher and people . . . In the best sense of the word, he is "possessed" – caught up in the message by the power of the Spirit. He becomes a channel used by the Holy Spirit.[27]

Spirit-anointed proclamation brings about a variety of emotions: awe (Luke 4:22), rage (Luke 4:28–29), conviction (Acts 2:37), ridicule (Acts 17:32), inquisitiveness (Acts 17:32), belief (Acts 17:34), and respect due to the authoritative nature of the proclamation (Matt 7:28–29). Anointing

---

23. Vines and Shaddix, *Progress in the Pulpit*, 76.
24. Azurdia, *Spirit Empowered Preaching*, 103, 107.
25. Heisler, *Spirit-led Preaching*, 138–141.
26. Heisler, *Spirit-led Preaching*, 138–141.
27. Vines and Shaddix, *Progress in the Pulpit*, 76, 77.

causes the preaching event to be a "Thus saith the Lord."[28] Preaching in the flesh is both difficult and wearisome, conversely anointed proclamation, depending on the Spirit, allows the message to ascend and provide results only the Spirit can accomplish. Anointing for the preacher and the listener is bread to the hungry and water to the thirsty. The modern pulpit does not talk about it or pursue it, but sadly diminishes, neglects, or dismisses the lifeline of effective preaching.[29]

To be sure, the Spirit is sovereign in what He does, but He has told us of various disciplines in the Word that He inspired that will allow His anointed touch in our preaching. Among them are:

1. a life given to *diligent study* (2 Tim 2:15 "*Do your best* to present yourself to God as one approved, a worker who has no need to be ashamed, rightly handling the word of truth").

2. a life given to *faith*. Vines and Shaddix provide parameters for this faithful Spirit-led ministry, "The anointing must be sought *day by day* in the pastor's walk with God, in his preparation process, and in each individual preaching event."[30]

3. a life that *fears God* more than man (2 Cor 5:11 "Therefore, knowing the *fear* of the Lord, we persuade others. But what we are is known to God, and I hope it is known also to your conscience").

4. a life given to the *glory* of God. Vines and Shaddix explain, "God has sovereignly ordained to unleash His strength through our weakness for reason – so no one steals His *glory!*"[31]

5. a life given to *holiness* (Heb 12:14 "Strive for peace with everyone, and for the *holiness* without which no one will see the Lord").

6. a life of *humility* (1 Pet 5:5 "Likewise, you who are younger, be subject to the elders. Clothe yourselves, all of you, with *humility* toward one another, for "God opposes the proud but gives grace to the humble").

---

28. Vines and Shaddix, *Progress in the Pulpit*, 36.

29. Vines and Shaddix, *Progress in the Pulpit*, 105. David Martyn Lloyd-Jones adds that "careful preparation and the unction of the Holy Spirit must never be regarded as alternatives, but as complementary to each other . . . Do you always look for and seek this unction, this anointing before preaching? Has this been your greatest concern? There is no more thorough and revealing test to apply to the preacher." Lloyd-Jones, *Preaching and Preachers*, 305.

30. Vines and Shaddix, *Progress in the Pulpit*, 108.

31. Vines and Shaddix, *Progress in the Pulpit*, 106.

7. a life given to *prayer* (Luke 18:1, "And he told them a parable to the effect that they ought always to *pray* and not lose heart").

8. a life of *pure motives* (Jas 4:8 "Draw near to God, and he will draw near to you. Cleanse your hands, you sinners, and *purify* your hearts, you double-minded").

9. a life of *preaching Christ* (1 Cor 1:23 "but we preach *Christ* crucified, a stumbling block to Jews and folly to Gentiles").[32]

10. a life that is *totally yielded* (Rom 6:13 "but *yield* yourselves unto God, as those that are alive from the dead, and your members as instruments of righteousness unto God – KJV").

Hershael W. York and Bert Decker are correct in affirming, "Although we cannot take the credit for the power and the presence of the Holy Spirit, we can usually take the blame for his absence."[33] Anointed much? Does your preaching look more like a performance or a proclamation? If the Holy Spirit was to withdraw from your preaching could your people tell the difference – could you? Did you even ask Him to fill you today?

> Proverbs 2:20 "So you will walk in the way of the good and keep to the *paths of the righteous.*"

> Prayer Point: Lord, forgive *me* for walking in the power of flesh, instead of the power of the Spirit. *My* lack of being Spirit-led in *my* personal walk, ministry, and proclamation is sin. You have placed Your Spirit within *me* – the power of God for holiness, ministry, and proclamation. May *I* truly begin to understand and live out that it is "Not by might, nor by power, but by my Spirit, says the Lord of hosts" (Zech 4:6).

---

32. Heisler, *Spirit-led Preaching*, 147–152.
33. York and Decker, *Preaching with Bold Assurance*, 8.

Chapter 7

A Mission-minded Ministry

"Wherefore he that would be a faithful minister of the Gospel must deny the pride of his heart, and be emptied of ambition, and set himself wholly to seek the glory of God in his calling."

— WILLIAM PERKINS[1] —

Acts 20:24 "But I do not account my life of any value nor as precious to myself, if only I may *finish my course* and the *ministry that I received* from the Lord Jesus, to testify to the gospel of the grace of God."

Commentary

Paul had just told this group of men from Ephesus something they no doubt understood but would still be a jarring revelation in Acts 20:23, namely, that he was headed toward certain "imprisonment and afflictions". However, in the next phrase, verse 24, we are given insight from Paul on exactly why he is able to persevere in the ministry as he declares, "But I do not account my life of any value nor as precious to myself." This phrase begins with the contrastive *"alla"* and indicates that Paul's answer to the expected difficulty and even prison time was that he did not consider his life on this earth to be worth being preserved at any cost. In this scenario death would

---

1. Perkins, *Commentary on Galatians*, 66.

be the worst thing Paul could expect but since his life held no value to him personally, he was willing to face whatever may come. Paul had concluded that, "Duty is of more importance than life; and when either duty or life is to be sacrificed, life is to be cheerfully surrendered."[2]

The Apostle Paul's view of the value of his own life was not an act of self-deprecation but, instead, a statement of means or intention. The following clause in verse 24 begins with the word "*hōs*" which is translated "if only." However, another translation that expresses the thought in this passage would be one of purpose such as "so that."[3] Therefore, Paul had a goal in mind for his view of his own life which was so "I may finish my course and the ministry." Paul's willingness to accept whatever hardship may come was purposeful, there was a goal, and it was a goal of completing what he saw as a race to accomplish. Ultimately, this course Paul saw laid before him was not one of accolades or fame but a role of service, indicated by his use of the word "*tēn diakonian*" translated "the ministry."

The origin of Paul's ministry is of such importance to him that he needs the Ephesian elders to know exactly from where his commission had come. The mission Paul had been given was a calling, not originating with his own desires or ambitions but, instead, he states it was one "that [he] received from the Lord Jesus." This was no ordinary calling but one that had come directly from the Lord Jesus Himself. The fact Paul had received his ministry from Jesus would also indicate that he saw himself as the steward of a mission with which he had been entrusted.

Paul's singular focus in life was to fulfill the ministry Jesus had given him and that mission was "to testify to the gospel of the grace of God." This act of testifying was the all-consuming activity of the Apostle's life whereby he intentionally and solemnly declared what he knew to be true to all those he encountered.[4] Not only was Paul intentional about the act of testifying but he was also specific regarding the message he was expressing, "the gospel of the grace of God." Paul's message was one of good news amid the tumult and destruction of sin and the subsequent judgment. "God's holiness and justice are like a great, violent hurricane, and the grace of God is like the eye of the hurricane where all is peace and calm. . . . Grace, or love, is the essential calm at the center of the vortex of his infinite perfections."[5]

---

2. Barnes, *Notes on the New Testament: Acts*, 293.
3. Louw–Nida, 784; BDAG, 1103.
4. BDAG, 233.
5. Piper, "A Cause to Live For," sect. 9–point 2.

A Mission-minded Ministry

This message of grace is one Paul had experienced firsthand and it was the sole purpose of his life and ministry to be a witness to this great message.

> Ministry Principle: we must be willing to die to self and remember it is the Lord Jesus's ministry in which He has allowed us to participate. Distractions abound but our objective has been clearly given and we must fulfill our calling . . . *we need a mission-minded ministry.*

A Portrait of a Mission-minded Ministry

At 18-years of age, I (Jeremy) moved away from home to begin my education at Criswell College in Dallas, Texas. Having moved from a small town outside of Houston, to say I was overwhelmed living on my own for the first time in the Dallas-Fort Worth Metroplex would be an understatement. The first thing on the list after moving into my apartment was to find a job and somewhere to serve in ministry and it would be great if I could find both in one position. The only thing I knew to do was take a long shot and reach out to a family friend who worked at First Baptist Church Dallas and see if there were any openings available. To my amazement, I was given an interview the next day for an intern position in the Missions Department with Dr. Lanny Elmore. I was extremely nervous so I don't really remember what I was asked or what I said but it must have gone well enough because he hired me.

The following year and half of my life was so formative it is hard to put into words. I learned personally from Dr. Elmore even more what it looked like to be a servant of God, preaching the Word, and ministering to the church. Watching Dr. Elmore minister and serve the people of God was second only to getting to know him personally as a minister, husband, father, grandfather, and Bible College professor. I once asked him what kept him going when things got difficult, when the people you serve don't like what you are attempting to do, or it seems to be making no effect. He responded with a story and, if you ever had the privilege of knowing the man, you would know this was a common occurrence.

When Lanny Elmore was in his early 20s, the Lord called him to plant a church in the hills of North Carolina. He did what the Lord asked and started a church with a handful of people. Early on, he struggled with the fact that he knew he had a mission the Lord had given him, and he wanted to fulfill it, but the church wasn't growing the way he thought it should and many Sundays there were only a few people who showed up. He had an old pulpit he preached from each service, and one week one of the men in the church came to him and said, "Come with me, I want to show you something." When they reached the pulpit, he noticed a small brass plaque that had been attached to it that only the one preaching could see and it said, "Preach preacher, God's listening!" This was the moment it all came into perspective for a young Lanny Elmore. The mission he had been given was given to him by the Lord and his calling was to give himself to that mission no matter the cost because God was the only One that he needed to please.

Years later, when I met him, Dr. Lanny Elmore had seemingly come a long way from that little church in the mountains to ministering in several churches, being a missionary for the International Mission Board in Uganda, earning his doctorate, and working for W.A. Criswell as the Missions Pastor of the First Baptist Church in Dallas, Texas where, for 27 years, he served faithfully, helping plant over 54 churches in over 12 languages. However, even after his "retirement," he served as the interim or transitional pastor for numerous churches and filled the pulpit at countless more until he physically could no longer. Throughout this amazing life of ministry, Dr. Elmore was one of the most grace-filled evangelists, sharing the gospel with people both from the pulpit and personally one-on-one.

With a ministry that spanned over 60 years, from the hills of North Carolina, to Africa, to First Baptist Dallas, Dr. Lanny Elmore was the epitome of one who put his mission to preach the gospel and serve the church at the forefront of his life. While it was a course filled with difficulty, hardship, loss, and frustration it was also a course marked with tremendous gospel work, countless souls coming to Christ, and he ran that course with fervor and faithfulness. God's servant, Lanny Elmore, entered the full presence of the Savior he served so faithfully on June 17, 2021. No doubt, when Dr. Elmore entered the presence of his Lord he heard, "Well done, good and faithful servant" as each of those in Christ will hear. In that moment he had finished the course and completed the mission the Lord had given him and with every last ounce of ability he had he fulfilled his calling. "Preach preacher, God's listening!" and calling His ministers to complete the mission they have been given for His glory.

A Mission to Prioritize

The ministry the Apostle Paul sought to complete, an endeavor he desired to accomplish so much it didn't matter if it claimed his life, was the mission to declare the good news of God's grace. Ministers will inevitably feel pressure to make numerous *other things* a priority in ministry. There will always be a tendency to want to *measure up* to the visible standards of growth whether that be the church's financial productivity, average numbers of baptisms, or worship attendance. It is important to note that none of these indicators is inherently negative, but they can be indicators of many different things. The issue with these three measures, or any other, is they are not the mission, they are not to be the priority we seek to accomplish. As ministers, we must prioritize the mission we have been given, we must be faithful to "testify to the gospel of the grace of God." Other facets of ministry are certainly important and may even be integral, but they are never the priority. The minister will feel pulled in many different directions and vital issues of ministry will take momentary precedence, and this is understandable, but nothing must ever be allowed to cloud, confuse, or cancel the primacy of his calling to preach the gospel of God's grace. The siren song to put even seemingly good tasks or accomplishments above the minister's principal calling will be the constant background track of daily ministry. However, the mission to preach the gospel must never take a back seat to anything, this testimony was the purpose of Paul's life, the minister's mission has not changed, and it is a mission that must be prioritized.[6]

A Mission to Complete

While rank and time have their place, for most long-distance runners, finishing is the absolute minimum requirement they place upon themselves. In fact, whether you are one or know one, if you ask a long-distance runner

---

6. While the priority of preaching the gospel should be ever in the forefront of the minister's mind this should, in no way, lead the minister to believe that the daily function of ministry should take precedence over his ministry of care, support, love, and spiritual guidance regarding family. The qualifications Paul gives Titus (Titus 1:5–9) and Timothy (1 Tim 3:1–13) show clearly that the Apostle understood the absolute need for the minister to have his family as his first ministry. However, this doesn't mean the ministry to "testify to the gospel of the grace of God" takes a secondary place, on the contrary, both 1 Timothy and Titus seem to show that the minister's first setting to preach and minister the gospel of God's grace is in the home.

how they feel after a race they didn't win, they may express disappointment in the place they finished, they may even speak about how they didn't hit the times they wanted to. Disappointment over rank or time is common, but speak to a long-distance runner who had to quit and not finish the course and you will have a completely different experience. Not accomplishing certain benchmarks will no doubt be accompanied with a certain level of 'letdown' but not finishing the race brings feelings of embarrassment and failure, merited or not, that are difficult to console.

The Apostle Paul referred to his willingness to "not account [his] life of any value" as the price he was ready to pay that "[he] may finish [his] course and the ministry." Notice Paul's focus, his sacrificial approach to life, was with the sole purpose of finishing the race or course that had been laid out before him. The mission of the minister, to expend fullness of life and energy to declare the gospel of the grace of God, like a marathon, is easy to begin but will take strength, training, and endurance to finish. However, the course before us is not one that is accomplished by starting brilliantly, it is not completed by quitting or being disqualified halfway through, it is only truly completed, and this may sound obvious, by finishing well. Just like the Apostle Paul, our sole desire should be to finish the race before us, the ministry to which we have been called, to give all we have to this mission, until we cross the finish line. Henry Martyn, missionary to India at the turn of the 19th century, just before his death in 1812 wrote:

> "And when I am dying how glad I shall be,
> That the lamp of my life has been blazed out for Thee.
> I shall not care in whatever I gave,
> Of labor or money one sinner to save.
> I shall not care that the way has been rough,
> That Thy dear feet led the way is enough.
> And when I am dying, how glad I shall be,
> That the lamp of my life has been blazed out for Thee."[7]

May we not only start strong but let us run faithfully and, when all our lives have been exhausted for the ministry of the gospel, may we "blaze out" for Him and complete the mission.

---

7. Quoted in Sanders, *Spiritual Maturity*, 154–155.

A Mission to Steward

Pride may be the most destructive tool of the enemy, especially among those in the ministry. Pride is what causes many to think the ministries they serve are anything other than an amazing stewardship given to them by the Lord. Pride is what can bring a minister to the place where he believes people should listen to him solely because of the title he carries, the degrees he has, or the position he occupies. Pride can cause a minister to believe his gifts of preaching, leadership, or administration are anything other than what they are . . . gifts from a gracious Father that are not evidence of the minister's worthiness but of the Father's glorious mercy. Therefore, understanding the ministry we have been given as a stewardship from our Lord and Savior and not one we birthed or formed is essential to battling the pride that can so easily creep in and destroy a ministry, leaving the course unfinished.

The Apostle Paul saw the ministry he had been given as a stewardship from Jesus Christ Himself. In the words of C.H. Spurgeon:

> Before his mind's eye he saw the Savior taking into His pierced hands the priceless case which contains the celestial jewel of the Grace of God and saying to him—"I have redeemed you with My blood and I have called you by My name—and now I commit this precious thing into your hands, that you may take care of it and guard it with your heart's blood. I commission you to go everywhere in My place and to make known to every people under Heaven the Gospel of the Grace of God.[8]

As we think about the ministry we may lead, we should always remember that it did not originate with us, nor does it belong to us in any way. Our calling is to take care of the ministry with which we have been entrusted and do so for the glory and praise of the One who gave it. Kings have inherent glory and majesty. However, a steward's authority or worth is only found in the King he serves and the value of the item or task with which he has been charged. May we never forget that our mission of ministry, the declaration of God's grace, is not of our making. We are recipients of a glorious gospel, we are conservators of a tremendous task, we are simply stewards of a Christ-given calling.

---

8. Spurgeon, "Gospel Worth Dying For," 1.

The Ministry We Need

A Mission with A Clear Message

Substitutes abound. Options are limitless. The minister can be drawn away in a myriad of directions from the primary message of his mission. In a desire to boost attendance, you may be tempted to preach a message of *self-help*. In a desire to not see attendance decline, you may be tempted to preach a message of *self-improvement* that emphasizes your hearer's ability to achieve their desired results in life (a better family life, a better career, a better financial situation) with just a little effort. In a desire to reach the sinful and secular culture, you may be tempted to preach a message of "easy-believism" that never forces the listener to confront their sinful state before a holy God. The Apostle Paul's mission was clear, our mission is clear, to *testify*, to give an accounting, to declare a message. The message we must declare destroys any hope of *self-help* or *self-improvement* because it is a message of mankind's absolute need for grace. The message we must declare is completely contrary to any concept of "easy-believism" because it is a message that forces mankind to face the reality of why it has an absolute need for grace.

While it can be easy when pressure mounts, to soften the hard truths of the message, to unhitch ourselves from the entirety of the message, or to gloss over the difficult portions of the message, our calling is made plain. When we "testify to the gospel of the grace of God" declare the individual's absolute brokenness and sin of mankind, both by nature (Rom 5:12–14), and by action (Rom 1:18–23). When we preach this message, we declare the complete guilt under which each person finds themselves (Rom 3:23). When we preach this message, we proclaim the provision God made through the person and work of Jesus Christ (1 Cor 15:3–5). When we testify to this message, we express that the foundation of this provision the Father has given is by grace alone and not based on any good within the individual (Eph 2:8–9). When we share this message, we herald the glorious gift of forgiveness and the Holy Spirit given to all those who repent and believe (Acts 2:38–39). When we proclaim this message, we preach the glorious eternal fellowship awaiting those who put their faith in Jesus Christ, alone, for their salvation (1 John 5:11). Our mission is to declare this message of God's grace. This is the mission we must prioritize. This is the mission we must complete. This is the mission we must steward well. This mission has a clear message of "the gospel of the grace of God." Let us devote ourselves to completing the mission we have been given and announce the good news of God's grace with urgency and faithfulness.

A Mission-minded Ministry

2 Timothy 4:5: "As for you, always be sober-minded, *endure* suffering, do the work of an evangelist, *fulfill* your ministry."

Prayer Point: Lord, forgive *me* where *I* have forgotten the mission You have given *me* and allowed other things to take precedence in *my* life. *My* desire is to fulfill the ministry You have placed before *me* and to declare the unsearchable riches of your grace until You call *me* home. Lord, grant *me* the grace to view this calling You have given *me* as more important even than *my* own life. Lord, may *I* complete the mission with which You have charged *me* by your grace and only for Your glory. Amen.

Chapter 8

A Blameless and Complete Ministry

*"There was a man in the land of Uz, whose name was Job;
and that man was blameless and upright,
and one who feared God and shunned evil."*

— JOB OF UZ 1:1 —

Acts 20:25–27 "And now, behold, I know that none of you among whom I have gone about proclaiming the kingdom will see my face again. Therefore I testify to you this day that *I am innocent of the blood of all*, for I did not shrink from *declaring to you the whole counsel of God.*"

Commentary

As Paul thought back on his ministry to the Ephesian church, he somehow felt like the watchman of Ezekiel 33:1–6:

> The word of the Lord came to me: "Son of man, speak to your people and say to them, If I bring the sword upon a land, and the people of the land take a man from among them, and make him their watchman, and if he sees the sword coming upon the land and blows the trumpet and warns the people, then if anyone who hears the sound of the trumpet does not take warning, and the sword comes and takes him away, his blood shall be upon his own head. He heard the sound of the trumpet and did not take

warning; his blood shall be upon himself. But if he had taken warning, he would have saved his life. But if the watchman sees the sword coming and does not blow the trumpet, so that the people are not warned, and the sword comes and takes any one of them, that person is taken away in his iniquity, *but his blood I will require at the watchman's hand.*

As far as Paul was concerned, he had faithfully finished his ministry there. He completed his God-given ministry assignment at Ephesus and believed he would never return to Asia Minor. There was the vast, untapped mission field of Rome and beyond to Spain. His powerful assertion of never returning makes the preceding words both solemn and extremely weighty.[1]

Many viewed Paul in Ephesus as an instigator and a religious usurper, but he makes an amazing statement that he is guilty of *no one's* blood there. Nobody's blood? Can that affirmation be true of much modern ministry? John Phillips asserts, "What a searching rebuke of much that passes for ministry in church today."[2] It begs us to look at our attitudes, actions, and witness to those who are outside of Christ. With his declaration of innocence before God analogous to the "Watchman" of Ezekiel 33, he turns his attention to the west. It is not the first time the Apostle filled the shoes of the Watchman. Declaring his mission to the Gentiles, Luke records at Corinth, "And when they opposed and reviled him, he shook out his garments and said to them, "Your blood be on your own heads! *I am innocent.* From now on I will go to the Gentiles"" (Acts 18:6).[3]

Paul sounded the *ram's horn* of the gospel; therefore, he had unburdened himself of the responsibility for those who have heard the message.[4] He has proclaimed the whole plan, the entire will of God, a thought-provoking

---

1. Phillips, *Exploring Acts*, 404. Kenneth Gangel asserts concerning the issue of whether in fact Paul did ever return to Ephesus, "Whether or not Paul was reflecting on his death or ministry plan Luke does not make it certain why Paul felt he would not return. The likelihood he did return is likely (2 Timothy 4:12) – but it does not change anything if that is what he felt." Gangel, *HNTC*, vol. 5, *Acts*, 342–343.

2. Phillips, *Exploring Acts*, 404.

3. Polhill, *NAC, Acts*, 426.

4. Charles Spurgeon speaks of this "unburdening" through the faithful proclamation of God's Word when he states, "Oh, my hearers, some of you in a little time will be on your dying beds. When your pulse is feeble; when the terrors of grim death are round about you; if you are still unconverted to Christ, there is one thing I shall want you to add to your last will and testament; it is this—the exclusion of the poor minister who stands before you this day from any share in that desperate folly of yours which has led you to neglect your own soul." Spurgeon, "The Minister's Farewell," sect. 2–para. 2.

phrase that includes gospel content and everything needed for Christian growth in sanctification.[5] Somehow his message of warning was complete to the extent that his message made him innocent before God of their blood. John MacArthur expands on this whole counsel or whole plan of God as:

> The entire purpose and plan of God for man's salvation in all its fullness: divine truths of creation, election, redemption, justification, adoption, conversion, sanctification, holy living, and glorification. Paul strongly condemned those who adulterate the Scripture (2 Cor 2:17; 2 Tim 4:3-4).[6]

As Paul left, he made the Ephesian elders accountable before God. They were to pick up where he left off – faithfully preaching the whole counsel of God and calling those who hear to repentance. Watchmen can do no more, for after the faithful sounding of the alarm, the responsibility falls to the hearers.[7]

> Ministry Principle: sadly today, many who occupy a pulpit stand accused of actions, activities, and attitudes that bring reproach to Christ and His church – in a moment, a ministry can face ruin, therefore what we need is a ministry that is a *blameless and complete* from start to finish.

A Portrait of a Blameless and Complete Ministry

Frankly, when I (Tony) think about a *blameless and complete* ministry, my list is short. In my mind, one calls for inclusion through longevity of faithfulness and integrity before God and His people. While there are few that make up my list, there is one individual who stands at the top – Dr. Jim Richards. He served for 21 years as a pastor in Louisiana, and then as a Director of Missions in Bentonville, Arkansas, and currently serves as the Executive Director Emeritus of the Southern Baptists of Texas Convention. I first met Dr. Richards at Woodforest Baptist Church in November 1998 at the inaugural meeting of the SBTC. He preached at my church for the first time in 2000 and I have gladly turned my pulpit over to him on many other occasions. I have seen him through interactions in my church, my home, in restaurants, in board meetings, and in denominational settings.

5. Gangel, *HNTC*, vol. 5, *Acts*, 342–343.
6. MacArthur, *One Faithful Life*, 335.
7. Polhill, *NAC, Acts*, 426.

A Blameless and Complete Ministry

Dr. Richards is a man of impeccable character, and, because of that he, would shun that characterization, for instead he would acknowledge there is only One of perfect impeccability. Nevertheless, he fulfills the *blameless* qualification. He would tell each of us as ministers that "only by the grace of God can one measure up to this . . . but he [the godly preacher] has a desire, a passion, a drive to want to be more like Jesus."[8] So, what are the foundational components of Dr. Richards's *blamelessness*? *First*, his unwavering stand for the Word of God. He and I were young men born of the Conservative Resurgence and his convictions are no passing fancy. In 1998, when the Baptist General Convention of Texas refused to affirm the new Baptist Faith and Message, he responded, "Some say Ephesians 5 is not relevant, so the issue is the nature of Scripture . . . we believe they are the words of God, that Scripture is the inerrant, infallible Word of God. The Word of God is absolute truth."[9] He goes on later in an article to the Baptist Press, "Without the trustworthiness of the Word of God, we have no ministry . . . the Word of God is all that we need as a sufficient guide to tell us how that we might in our ministry be proficient and how that we might serve [God] to please him."[10] He reminds all ministers and God's church, "For those who get weary of hearing about battles for the Bible, let me remind you that eternal vigilance is necessary to preserve the truth. The battle for the Bible will never be over until Jesus returns."[11] *Another truth that drives this blameless outcome is the call of God on his life:*

> God's supernatural call upon our life is inexplicable. There is no way that we can measure it, no way that we can somehow categorize it, but it is nevertheless a valid and genuine experience, the calling of God . . . oh, we may falter and we may fall and we may stumble and we'll definitely make mistakes and errors, and even sin, but if he's called you, he'll enable you to carry out the task.[12]

While some allegedly *stand* for the Word, their actions and attitudes do not match their beliefs. Dr. Richards is always gracious in his application of truth, "While injustices call for prophets, problems should be dealt with in a Christ-like spirit. Disagreements should be handled in Christian

---

8. Richards, "Seeking Direction in the Church," 17:33.
9. Hinkle, "Southern Baptists of Texas Mark Ongoing Hikes," para. 3.
10. Hailey, "Christians Need to Be 'Marked for Ministry,'" para. 2–3.
11. Richards, "Easter: The Essential Resurrection," para. 2.
12. Hailey, "Christians Need to Be 'Marked for Ministry,'" line 29–31, 37–38.

dialogue, not derogatory accusations."[13] This Christ-like spirit stems from his personal holiness, "God has called us to walk in his way. That means separated from sin. He is calling us to holiness, and I fear what has happened is we've become slackers in our Christian walk."[14]

Early in my ministry I worked with a Director of Missions who incessantly treated me with disrespect both in word and deed. While my age and stance within the convention may have contributed to his contempt, his disdain was due in large part to the fact I pastored in his mind a small and insignificant church. While I still pastor a comparatively small church, Dr. Richards (albeit an Executive Director for 20-plus years), treats me with the utmost respect – he returns my calls, he answers my texts and emails, and he has allowed me to serve in roles I would not otherwise have ever dreamt of serving in. He consistently practices what he preaches, delivering a ministry that is both *blameless and complete*:

> 1 Timothy 2:2 – 'What you have heard from me in the presence of many witnesses entrust to faithful men who will be able to teach others also', Paul told Timothy. This should be your legacy! . . . Believers have a legacy to pass on to the next generation and God wants us to hand off a gospel legacy to the next generation. Relationships and the revelation of God's Word are the two influences we have to promote that gospel legacy.[15]

He speaks of a gospel legacy to pass on and I know firsthand he believes this because both my two sons are senior pastors and he has preached in their churches, served on one's doctoral dissertation committee, invited them to preach and serve in denominational positions, and has loved their families. Dr. Richards himself sums up what a *blameless and complete* ministry looks like:

> If I were to speak to a pastor who is beginning his ministry, the *one* item that I would consider the most important is a personal walk with God. If a pastor doesn't have a personal private time with God through prayer and scripture, if there's not that interaction in the Spirit, if there is not a quiet time and alone time with God then that pastor can't possibly survive with his family, with his church or with any extra church ministry. So, it is essential for the pastor to have that personal walk with God. But I would go further to say

---

13. Richards, "Baptist Center for Theology and Ministry interview," pg. 1–question 2.
14. Hailey, "Christians Need to Be 'Marked for ministry,'" line 43–45.
15. Richards, "Annual Meeting 2018," 03:50 and 04:35.

that if there's one thing that I would say to a pastor beyond that, *number two* would be to have that family relationship. The ministry begins with the family, not the church. A pastor could have a quote "successful pastorate" and lose his family. It's essential that he keep his family a priority in his affections and attention. And then of course, the church ministry would be *third* and then *fourth* anything beyond the local church. So, the one great thing is, walk with God and all the rest will fall in place.[16]

Blameless and Complete – Persevering in His Character and Ministry

When one is considering a *blameless and complete* ministry, the word perseverance comes to mind. Some may view perseverance as a patient exercise in passivity, but nothing could be further from the truth. To persevere means to endure actively and victoriously, still being faithful to the Lord no matter what happens. A *blameless and complete* ministry therefore, for our purposes means to endure actively and victoriously, remaining faithful to the Lord in our character, ministry, witness and preaching no matter what happens. The preacher who is *blameless and complete* is a man who allows the gospel to shape his life and ministry. He is more akin to John the Baptist than a CEO, walking in a holy boldness that sets him apart from the world. People look at him and say, he is not only qualified (1 Tim 3:1–7; Titus 1:5–9) but God has made him into a new creation, "The old has passed away; behold, the new has come" (2 Cor 5:17).

But it begs the question, "Is there anyone that is *blameless*?" Some confuse blameless with faultless, certainly the blameless man is not perfect. Blameless (*anenkletos*) is literally, "without accusation." The blameless minister is one who no one can bring a charge against. This word serves as the umbrella term that covers all the elder's life. The following scriptures detail his blamelessness (1 Tim 3:2; Titus 1:7) and reflect his relationships to God, His Word, self, family, others including the outside world, and to possessions.

There cannot be a discussion about a ministry that is *blameless and complete* without discussing the character of the preacher. He truly must practice what he preaches, modeling through his character the truth he

---

16. Richards, "What Is the One Thing," 00:19.

proclaims.[17] Stephen and David Olford are right, "God is more concerned with *what we are* than with *what we do*. If *what we are* does not satisfy His holy demands, then *what we do* is virtually worthless."[18] Paul seizes his young protégé Timothy's attention by designating him as the "man of God" – one who is in God's service, represents God & speaks in His name. It is used of Moses (Deut 33:1), Samuel (1 Sam 9:6), Elijah (1 Kgs 17:24), and Elisha (2 Kgs 4:7), and is only used in the New Testament to describe Timothy and those who follow him (2 Tim 3:17). Paul declares in 1 Timothy 6:11, "But as for you, O *man of God*, flee these things. Pursue righteousness, godliness, faith, love, steadfastness, gentleness." Along with these six pursuits as the *man of God*, he is also to "set the believers an example in *speech*, in *conduct*, in *love*, in *faith*, in *purity*" (1 Tim 4:12). One can clearly see these qualities fleshed out in the pastoral qualifications of 1 Timothy 3:1–7 and Titus 1:5–9.

Scripture reminds us repeatedly of the importance of our words and our *speech*. "The tongue of the wise commends knowledge, but the mouths of fools pour out folly" (Prov 15:2). As preachers we forget sometimes that we are only heralds in what we preach (it is God's message, not ours) and witnesses to what we have seen and heard (not our opinions or outbursts). Our speech is to be blameless (1 Tim 3:2; Titus 1:7), self-controlled, sensible, respectable, hospitable (1 Tim 3:2), not quick tempered, not quarrelsome, not arrogant, not controlled by alcohol (1 Tim 3:3; Titus 1:7). When our tongues fail us, God's Word reminds us that it is our heart that failed us first – "Keep your heart with all vigilance, for from it flow the springs of life" (Prov 4:23) and "For out of the abundance of the heart the mouth speaks" (Matt 12:34).

Like Paul warned Timothy to watch his words, he also admonished him to live in such a way that exemplified Christ. His lifestyle or *conduct* was to be blameless, above reproach (1 Tim 3:2; Titus 1:7). He is to be hospitable, loving what is good, sensible, righteous, holy, self-controlled, gentle (1 Tim 3:3; Titus 1:8). He is to not be arrogant, not hot-tempered, not an excessive drinker, not a bully and not greedy for money (1 Tim 3:3; Titus 1:7). His conduct must be upright and his home an example to all in the way he cares for and loves his wife (1 Tim 3:2; Titus 1:6) and in the way he parents his children (1 Tim 3:4; Titus 1:6). Paul draws an obvious conclusion – if a man cannot care for and be an example in his own little family,

---

17. Prime and Begg, *On Being a Pastor*, 37.
18. Olford and Olford, *Anointed Expository Preaching*, 3.

how then will he care for and be an example to God's larger family, the church (1 Tim 3:5)? He is to reflect God not only to those within the house of God, but those outside as well (1 Tim 3:7).

The third way that the man of God should be an example, as Paul said, is *in love*. Love ought to highlight every area of his life. He is to be above reproach in that love characterizes his life (1 Tim 3; Titus 1:7). He is to love strangers through hospitality, love the good, exude righteous love, holy love and a love that is self-controlled and gentle (1 Tim 3:3; Titus 1:8). By comparison, he is not to love alcohol, anger, arrogance, a combative spirit, or money (1 Tim 3:3; Titus 1:7). He is to love his wife and children in such a way that it translates positively to how he lovingly pastors his church (1 Tim 3:2; Titus 1:6) and this will be readily clear to God's people and those outside of the church (1 Tim 3:7). I have often heard it said by preachers, "oh, I would love pastoring if it were not for the people," how sad that is. Peter commanded God's shepherds to "shepherd the flock of God that is among you, exercising oversight, not under compulsion, but *willingly*, as God would have you; not for shameful gain, but *eagerly*" (1 Pet 5:2). The implication here is that it is willingly *because you love them*. Ministers who neglect to conduct themselves *in love* are really behaving as the unregenerate (Matt 5:46–47).

Often in Scripture, we find faith and love coupled together. On no less than 10 occasions, Paul mentions this couplet to Timothy (1 Tim 1:5, 14; 2:15; 4:12; 6:11; 2 Tim 1:13; 2:22; 3:10). In these texts, the preacher is encouraged to have a sincere faith, an overflowing faith, a faith that continues, be an example in *faith*, a faith that is pursued, a faith that holds to sound teaching, and a faith that follows godly examples. So, faith is something the preacher *possesses* but also something he should *pursue*; it is the means of his justification, sanctification, and one day will find fulfillment in glorification. It is also that affirmed body of truth that Jude calls "the faith" (Jude 3). The preacher must know it, to be able to teach it to those who hear and refute false teaching (Titus 1:9; 1 Tim 3:2).

Finally, the man of God is to "set the believers an example in *speech*, in *conduct*, in *love*, in *faith*, in *purity*" (1 Tim 4:12). Holiness – what once broke our heart, we now laugh at; what once brought us shame, we now excuse. "My people's greatest need is my personal holiness" and "How awful a weapon in the hand of God is a holy minister."[19] Would to God that it could

---

19. Often attributed to M'Cheyne there is no verification in his writings, although he spoke often about holiness. Whether he said these words or not, it does not minimize the

be said of us as it was of Elisha, "I know that this is a *holy man* of God who is continually passing our way" (2 Kgs 4:9). As with the other characteristics, the man of God's purity must be above reproach (1 Tim 3:2; Titus 1:6). He must be faithful to his wife in every way. All interaction with the opposite sex must be above suspicion and the wise minister will avoid all situations where he or his testimony can suffer compromise. A lawyer can still practice law even if he is unfaithful to his wife, a doctor can practice medicine if he lives an impure lifestyle, but the *man of God* must walk in purity or else forfeit the privilege of ministry.

The office of the pastor is not simply something one fills for the standards are as high and sacred as God's Word reveals. Jared Wilson speaks to this, "Beyond giftedness and ambition, it requires maturity, testing, and a long obedience in the same direction. Because of this, when a pastor has become disqualified ... the leadership office demands a higher standard.[20] *Can the man of God who has violated his purity or participated in some other egregious act find restoration to fellowship?* The answer to that is clear (Matt 18:15–35; 2 Cor 2:5–11; Gal 6:1), but there are other necessary questions. Any believer who has sinned (including a pastor) can and should find restoration in the church, following they have adhered to the repentant process set forth by the church. A second and necessary question is *Can a disqualified pastor become restored or requalified?*[21] Some cite Jesus's restoration of Peter – not just to fellowship, but also to leadership (*feed my sheep* ...).[22] If one grants legitimacy to this answer, then a third vital

---

two truth's potency. Prime and Begg, *On Being a Pastor*, 35.

20. Wilson, "Thoughts on the Restoration," para. 5. A full discussion of this is beyond the scope of this chapter. There are numerous opinions, may each of ours be biblically informed.

21. A Lifeway Research poll asked, "If a pastor commits adultery, how long should they withdraw from public ministry?" The answers? 1) Not at all 2 percent, 2) Less than one year 6 percent, 3) At least one year 16 percent, 4) At least 2 to 10 years 18 percent, 5) Permanently 27 percent, and 6) Not sure 31 percent. While the poll is enlightening, the fact that almost one-third answered, "Not sure," speaks to either the difficulty of the question, the ignorance of the question, or the unwillingness to address the question. Earls, "Restoration, Return Unclear for Adulterous Pastors," chart after para. 3.

22. While he would agree that a repentant leader's restoration to fellowship can and should be the case, Dr. Richard Land (former president of the ERLC) would disagree with a restoration to leadership. When asked, "Should fallen Christian leaders be allowed to return to ministry," he answers, "When someone with effective, "de facto" pastoral oversight and responsibility (not only pastors and church staff, but also teachers in Christian schools and colleges, especially coaches and religion and Bible teachers, and para-church ministers who serve through Cru, InterVarsity, Ratio Christi, etc.) has betrayed their

question follows, "*How soon can restoration and requalification take place?*" If one arrives at this point in the discussion, the answer is *later*, not *sooner*; it is a process. We need to remember:

- Discerning godly grief is necessary (John 21:7; 2 Cor 7:10). While the church is not omniscient, she is the determiner (through the means of the Word and the Spirit) of the genuineness of this grief.
- Restoration to the fellowship is different from restoration to the pastorate.
- Peter did not restore himself (*neither do pastors today*) – Jesus did. Jesus is not here, but the church, as Christ's representative, affirms or disqualifies men to the office of pastor based on biblical criteria.
- Forgiveness is immediate upon repentance – trust, however, is seldom immediate.
- No man is greater than the church of the living God. "The gospel is not expendable. But our ministries are."[23]

These are the areas of our example before believers – it is a part of our sacred trust before God. Paul reminded the Ephesian elders to "*Pay careful attention to yourselves* and to all the flock, in which the Holy Spirit has made you overseers, to care for the church of God, which he obtained with his own blood" (Acts 20:28). In an age of political correctness, godless standards, and sin without consequences, the man of God must not buy what the culture is selling. Yes, there is a wideness in God's mercy, but there is no margin for error in our purity, "But I discipline my body and keep it under control, *lest after preaching to others I myself should be disqualified*" (1 Cor 9:27). Christ has set the way as an example *in speech, in conduct, in love, in faith,* and *in purity.* "And being found in human form, he humbled himself by becoming obedient to the point of death, even death on a cross" (Phil 2:8)—While most of us will not have to die for our obedience, the real

---

sacred trust, can they ever again be trusted with that kind of ministry role by Christian leaders who have the responsibility to protect God's people from false shepherds? I believe that the answer must be a resounding, "no!" Why? When people betray the sacred and holy trust bestowed upon them by Christian leaders, their potential restoration must be trumped by Christian leaders' sacred duty to protect those ministered to and who have been betrayed. It should always be remembered that "the best predictor of future performance is past behavior." Land, "Ask Dr. Land: Should Fallen Christian Leaders Be Allowed to Return to Ministry?" para. 5–6.

23. Wilson, "Thoughts on the Restoration," last paragraph.

question then is "Are you willing to live in obedience, to be above reproach in all things?"

If the qualities of a preacher are *blameless*, it would be logical to assume that the out-workings of that in the man's ministry would be *blameless* as well. His passion for the Word of God would be self-evident as he seeks "first the kingdom of God and his righteousness" (Matt 6:33). He will not simply study for sermons but will have as his goal an audience with the King. He will not find satisfaction in feeding his people left-overs, husks, and chaff for "what has straw in common with wheat?" (Jer 23:28). Instead, he will "speak my word faithfully" (Jer 23:28) for the Lord says of His Word "is not my word like fire . . . and like a hammer that breaks the rock in pieces?" (Jer 23:29). The Lord renders a verdict on less than blameless ministry – "For the shepherds are stupid and do not inquire of the Lord" (Jer 10:21).

Paul typifies a *blameless* ministry. At the end of his life, he writes "I have fought the good fight, I have finished the race, I have kept the faith" (2 Tim 4:7). To be blameless is to passionately fight the good fight of faith against the world (1 John 2:15), the flesh (Rom 7:14–24), and the devil (Eph 6:10–18). Leonard Ravenhill enlightens us on many a preacher's passion, "The church right now has more fashion than passion, is more pathetic than prophetic, is more superficial than supernatural." *Blameless and complete* means finishing the race. Fallen ministers litter the pastoral landscape, a grim reminder of those who do not finish well and end up making shipwreck of their testimony. Ministers are stewards of a sacred task for, "it is required of stewards that they be found faithful" (1 Cor 4:2).

Finally, the man of God must keep the faith. This is both *propositional* (be faithful to the faith once delivered to the saints) and *personal* (live out the faith once delivered to the saints). It was carefully passed to us:

> Now I would remind you, brothers, of the gospel I preached to you, *which you received*, in which you stand, and by which you are being saved, if you hold fast to the word I preached to you—unless you believed in vain. For I *delivered to you* as of first importance what I also received: that Christ died for our sins in accordance with the Scriptures, that he was buried, that he was raised on the third day in accordance with the Scriptures" (1 Cor 15:1–4).

How are we overseeing that precious message, both in proclamation and life? Usually, we think of blameless concerning the big-ticket items such as moral failure, adultery, indecency, pornography, sexual abuse, embezzling money, and "sexual immorality among you, and of a kind that is not tolerated even among pagans" (1 Cor 5:1). But what about lying on a résumé, plagiarizing sermon material, idiotic Tweets or posts on Facebook, or even not returning phone calls or emails? Surely D. L. Moody is correct, "There are many of us who are willing to do great things for the Lord, but few of us are willing to do little things." We are to live above reproach before man, our family, the church and most importantly to God. The warning has sounded for the man of God, "Not many of you should become teachers, my brothers, for you know that we who teach will be judged with greater strictness" (Jas 3:1). Paul confirms James's truth:

> For we must all appear before the judgment seat of Christ, so that each one may receive what is due for what he has done in the body, whether good or evil. Therefore, knowing the fear of the Lord, we persuade others. But what we are is known to God, and I hope it is known also to your conscience (2 Cor 5:10–11).

An ominous proposition for the pastor who is not *blameless*. For the man of God who is *blameless* to the end, *completing* his ministry, he can gladly say, "there is laid up for me the crown of righteousness, which the Lord, the righteous judge, will award to me on that day, and not only to me but also to all who have loved his appearing" (2 Tim 4:8).

Blameless and Complete – Persevering in Expository Preaching

The starting point for a *blameless and complete* ministry as preaching the whole counsel of God begins with an understanding of expository preaching. First, God has spoken. As one reads the repeated pattern in Genesis 1 "And God said" (vv. 3, 6, 9, 11, 14, 20, 24, 26), the reader quickly perceives the importance of God speaking and thus revealing things about Himself. The ground of expository preaching is the conviction that God spoke and continues to do so through His Word; this same *Word* God breathes out (2 Tim 3:16) and therefore what God has revealed the preacher must declare and proclaim. This *breathed-out truth* demands correct handling from the study to the pulpit (2 Tim 2:15), in private counsel and corporate worship.[24] H. B. Charles summarizes the importance of expository preaching and God's revealed truth:

---

24. Charles, *On Pastoring*, 157.

> The reason why you should be a student of expository preaching is not about a style of preaching. What you preach is infinitely more important than how you preach. The act of preaching is in vain if the message preached is not true. Paul charged Timothy, 'Preach the Word' (2 Tim. 4:2a). He did not charge Timothy to simply preach, as if the function of preaching has any power of its own.[25]

In the end, the preacher's charge to care for God's people includes feeding and leading (Acts 20:28); if the preacher has no confidence that God has spoken and continues to do so, authority is undermined and there will be no sense of urgency in his preaching.[26]

With preaching, and preaching the whole counsel of God, comes the understanding that God's Word faithfully proclaimed supplies *information*, *transformation,* and *formation* for the believer. Peter reveals this magnificent truth:

> His divine power has granted to us *all things that pertain to life and godliness*, through the knowledge of him who called us to his own glory and excellence, by which he has granted to us his precious and very great promises, so that through them you may become partakers of the divine nature, having escaped from the corruption that is in the world because of sinful desire (2 Pet 1:3-4).

Jerry Vines and Jim Shaddix tell us that "the apostle Paul claimed the Word of grace will foster spiritual growth and advance the believer toward glorification (Acts 20:32)."[27] We preach to the lost and to believers on every spectrum of sanctification – it is the aroma of life for the saved and the stench of death to the perishing (2 Cor 2:14-15), therefore our preaching must be faithful, clear and persuasive.[28] Confidence in the entirety of God's Word is paramount for it is clear that *the man of God* has the responsibilities to *feed* the flock (1 Pet 5:2), *present* believers under his care as mature or perfect in Christ (Col 1:28-29), *prepare* God's people to "do" ministry (Eph 4:12), *equip* them to lead people to Christ, and to finish the job that God gave him (Acts 20:24).

If we are to be *blameless and complete* in our preaching, we are going to be sure to preach and teach the entirety of God's Word. Paul provides specific and expanded information to his young protégé (2 Tim 3:10-17).

---

25. Charles, *On Pastoring*, 141.
26. Vines and Shaddix, *Progress in the Pulpit*, 65.
27. Vines and Shaddix, *Progress in the Pulpit*, 68.
28. Charles, *On Pastoring*, 154.

He appeals to Timothy to 1) *follow* the pattern of his teaching and conduct (2 Tim 3:10–11), 2) *see* truth as a necessity, for the church will face persecution and false teachings (2 Tim 3:12–13), 3) *understand* that the only answer is in the *sacred writings* – all of them "All Scripture is inspired by God and is profitable or useful (2 Tim 3:16). Therefore, "all Scripture" (2 Tim 3:16) is parallel to the "whole counsel" (Acts 20:27) of God.[29] This "all Scripture (*pasa graphē*)" – is altogether "breathed out by God." The goal is so the "man of God may be complete, equipped for every good work" (2 Tim 3:17). The implication for preaching the *whole counsel of God* and *all Scripture* is that the preacher must communicate the Word of God entirely as God Himself gave it. So, what exactly did Paul intend for the modern preacher to cover in his preaching ministry when he said, "I did not shrink from declaring to you the whole counsel of God"?

There is a link between preaching the whole counsel of God and Paul's two imperatives for preachers to *"follow the pattern of the sound words* that you have heard from me, in the faith and love that are in Christ Jesus. By the Holy Spirit who dwells within us, *guard the good deposit* entrusted to you" (2 Tim 1:13–14).[30] It is through achieving the goal of verse 27 to preach the whole counsel of God that Paul can declare himself innocent of their blood, verse 26. Tony Merida suggests three crucial questions to ask if one wants to be faithful in preaching the whole counsel of God – *"What is the Bible about? Is there a unified message in Scripture? Is the same God revealed in both testaments?*[31] If the preacher does not understand these basic answers, he will not see the one message of the Bible, nor will he see fit to preach the Bible in its entirety for *all Scripture* and *whole counsel* will only be true in theory and not in practice.

One can translate *counsel* (*boulēn*) as will, purpose, or plan. When associated with God, especially in the Luke/Acts narratives, it speaks of God's grand purpose of redemption through the death and resurrection of Christ

---

29. Richard Mayhue expands this thought even further by stating that "The spirit of expository preaching is exemplified in two biblical texts: They read from the book, from the law of God, translating to give the sense so that they understood the reading" (Neh. 8:8)" and the text for this chapter Acts 20:26–27. Mayhue, "Rediscovering Expository Preaching," 13.

30. That Paul goes to such pains, it may suggest the temptation for ministers to not preach the whole counsel of God's will – i.e., verse 21 "testifying both to Jews and to Greeks of repentance toward God and of faith in our Lord Jesus Christ." – the important example is repentance – a priority principle taught to both unbelievers and believers. Prime and Begg, *On Being a Pastor*, 50.

31. Merida, *Faithful Preaching*, 40.

that leads to that gospel message faithfully proclaimed among the nations. It corresponds to "to testify to the gospel of God's grace" and "proclaiming the kingdom" in the earlier verses (Acts 20:24–25) and to "the word of his grace, which is able to build you up and to give you the inheritance among all those who are sanctified" which follows (Acts 20:32). It is to preach from Genesis to Revelation all of God's salvation in Christ:

> For those whom he foreknew he also predestined to be conformed to the image of his Son, in order that he might be the firstborn among many brothers. And those whom he predestined he also called, and those whom he called he also justified, and those whom he justified he also glorified" (Rom 8:29–30).

It is not simply enough to preach the *counsel* of God but the *whole counsel* of God. *Whole* (*pasan*) modifies counsel to be entirely complete (hence *blameless and complete*). Therefore, it is neither partial nor selective, for Paul used all the sacred Scriptures at his disposal. We find Paul's ministry of the Word to the Ephesians summarized in this way:

> This continued for two years, so that all the residents of Asia heard the word of the Lord, both Jews and Greeks . . . How I did not shrink from declaring to you anything that was profitable, and teaching you in public and from house to house . . . Therefore be alert, remembering that for three years I did not cease night or day to admonish every one with tears (Acts 19:10; 20:20; 31).

The man of God *should* never run out of material to preach (he has all the Word of God) – the man of God *should* never be afraid to preach all the Word of God (it is all inspired) – the man of God *should* strive to preach God's whole counsel (we are heralds of all His revelation).

According to Acts 20:27, we as the men of God are under divine obligation to preach "the whole counsel of God." John Piper rightly concludes, "But we look more and more to the professional academicians for books which fit the jagged pieces or revelation into a unified whole . . . we have, by and large, lost the Biblical vision of a pastor as one who is mighty in the Scriptures, apt to teach, competent to confute opponents, and able to penetrate to the unity of the whole counsel of God."[32] The process of hearing and believing the whole counsel of God so that one may preach it is part of the godly heritage of the "man of God" as Paul told Timothy, "What you have heard from me in the presence of many witnesses entrust to faithful

---

32. Piper, *Brothers, We Are Not Professionals*, 84.

men, who will be able to teach others also" (2 Tim 2:2). We see a clear picture of the purpose and the end of the whole counsel of God at work in the life of Apollos in Acts 18:24–28. While he walked in the light he had, he needed further light, he needed the full counsel of God:

> Now a Jew named Apollos, a native of Alexandria, came to Ephesus. He was an eloquent man, competent in the Scriptures. He had been instructed in the way of the Lord. And being fervent in spirit, he spoke and taught accurately the things concerning Jesus, *though he knew only the baptism of John*. He began to speak boldly in the synagogue, but when Priscilla and Aquila heard him, *they took him aside and explained to him the way of God more accurately*. And when he wished to cross to Achaia, the brothers encouraged him and wrote to the disciples to welcome him. When he arrived, he greatly helped those who through grace had believed, for *he powerfully refuted the Jews in public, showing by the Scriptures that the Christ was Jesus*.

We are living in a time of famine akin to the prophet Amos:

> Behold, the days are coming," declares the Lord God, "when I will send a famine on the land—not a famine of bread, nor a thirst for water, *but of hearing the words of the Lord*. They shall wander from sea to sea, and from north to east; they shall run to and fro, to seek the word of the Lord, but they shall not find it (Amos 8:11–12).

The best way to satisfy this hunger is through the exposition of the whole counsel of God. H. B. Charles reveals two reasons for a commitment to expository preaching and the whole counsel of God, "On one hand, *I am not smart enough to preach* anything but the Bible. On the other hand, *I am too smart to preach* anything but the Bible."[33] Finally, there are consequences of not preaching the whole counsel of God – 1) one might end up with the practical belief that there is a *canon within the canon*, 2) the congregation might end up with a narrow or imbalanced theology (especially a narrow gospel), and 3) the congregation might never grasp the overall message and shape of the Scriptures.[34] John Piper adds to this, "If we do not unfold "the whole counsel of God" (Acts 20:27), then we encourage drifting downstream where they will make shipwreck of their faith (1 Tim. 1:19)."[35] We desperately need ministries that are *blameless and complete*. In the end

---

33. Charles, *On Pastoring*, 143.
34. Patrick and Reid, *Whole Counsel of God*, 76–79.
35. Piper, *Brothers, We Are Not Professionals*, 110.

our goals are faithful lives and the faithful unfolding of the whole counsel of God through expository preaching, for as Derek J. Prime and Alistair Begg say, we will "avoid emphases that make us unhelpfully distinctive because of particular axes we are known to grind."[36]

> Genesis 17:1 When Abram was ninety-nine years old the Lord appeared to Abram and said to him, "I am God Almighty; walk before me, and be *blameless*."

James 1:4 "And let steadfastness have its full effect, that you may be perfect and *complete*, lacking in nothing."

> Prayer Point: Lord, *I* acknowledge *my* weakness – *I* can do nothing without You. May *I* live *my* life in such a way, may *my* actions and attitudes honor You, so that You, God may find *me blameless*, as well as those *I* serve. May *I* persevere through the days, weeks, months, years, and decades to present to You a *complete* ministry.

---

36. Prime and Begg, *On Being a Pastor*, 51.

Chapter 9

A Vigilant Ministry

"A good shepherd is always alert to danger. He is not caught unaware.
He is vigilant and ready to act in order to protect the sheep."
— ALEXANDER STRAUCH[1] —

Acts 20:28–31 "Pay careful attention to yourselves and to all the flock, in which the Holy Spirit has made you overseers, to care for the church of God, which He obtained with His own blood. I know that after my departure fierce wolves will come in among you, not sparing the flock; and from among your own selves will arise men speaking twisted things, to draw away the disciples after them. Therefore be alert, remembering that for three years I did not cease night or day to admonish every one of you with tears."

Commentary

In sobering fashion, the Apostle Paul sounds the alarm for vigilance among the Ephesian elders in Acts 20:28–31. He begins the call with a command, "Pay careful attention...." Take note of the present imperative, *"prosechete,"* which indicates to every pastor the ever-present call for vigilance in ministry. Though a three-word phrase in English, the Greek employs only one

---

1. Strauch, *Biblical Eldership*, 152.

"*prosechete*," which speaks of a continuous state of readiness to learn of any future danger, need, or error in order to respond appropriately, and can be translated, "to pay attention to, keep on the lookout for, be alert for, be on one's guard for." Every pastor needs to read Paul's exhortation afresh and rouse themselves to be on guard. Distractions abound and the flesh is always desirous of leisure and indifference, but what we need is vigilant pastors carrying out vigilant ministry.

In verse 28, we see Paul's imperative, "Pay careful attention" applied in two directions, "to yourselves and to all the flock...." First, we examine what it is for an elder *to pay careful attention to himself*. Paul instructed Timothy in similar fashion, writing, "Keep a close watch on yourself and on the teaching. Persist in this, for by so doing you will save both yourself and your hearers" (1 Tim 4:16). Timothy, and all pastors in like manner, was commanded to watch closely over himself. Surely, the command applies to watching over one's integrity and morality, being eager to abide in Christ (John 15:4) and remaining ever qualified to continue in the work of the ministry (1 Tim 3:1–7, Titus 1:5–9). A pastor must guard against his own destruction, even his own self-destruction. Read the words of Richard Baxter:

> Take heed to yourselves because the tempter will make his first and sharpest attack on you . . . he knows what devastation he is likely to make among the rest if he can make the leaders fall before their eyes. He has long practiced fighting, neither against great nor small, comparatively, but against the shepherds—that he might scatter the flock . . . Take heed, then, for the enemy has a special eye on you. You are sure to have his most subtle insinuations, incessant solicitations and violent assaults. Take heed to yourselves, lest he outwit you. The devil is a greater scholar than you are, and a more nimble disputant . . . and whenever he prevails against you, he will make you the instrument of your own ruin . . . Do not allow him to use you as the Philistines used Samson—first to deprive you of your strength, then put out your eyes, and finally to make you the subject of his triumph and derision.[2]

Secondly, we examine what it is for an elder *to pay careful attention to the flock*. Here, the church is figuratively referred to as the "flock," "*poimniō*," that is, the people of God who follow the Good Shepherd, the Lord Jesus (John 10:11,14). Elders have been made overseers of the local church by none other than the Holy Spirit. As stewards and overseers of Jesus's

---

2. Baxter, *The Reformed Pastor*, 7.

blood-bought people, we have a responsibility *to pay careful attention* to their spiritual well-being. An *overseer*, *"episkopous,"* which is plural in this passage, is a "curator, guardian, superintendent" with the responsibility *to care for*, the flock which carries the idea of leading, with an implication of provision. Elders are responsible for tending to the needs of the members of the church, especially the spiritual needs. If the shepherds of a local church fail to tend to the flock, the flock will suffer great harm. Caring for the flock is achieved by what shepherds provide for the people and by the shepherds fending off *the fierce wolves* who would seek to abuse and prey on God's people.

Paul warns the Ephesian elders that in their care for the people of God they must be vigilant to fend off *wolves* (v. 29). These wolves are described as *fierce*, *"bareis"* which describes something that is vicious, cruel, and savage. Wolves have no regard for the lives of their victims. Wolves tear and devour to satisfy their appetites and make no calculation as to the value of their victims beyond what they can receive from them. The shepherds of a local church must be on the alert for wolves that come from the outside and those that arise from the inside. We read this in Paul's words, as he says, "Fierce wolves will come in among you," that is, from the outside. People who would abuse the church spiritually, physically, and financially will indeed come from outside the church, making no pretense of spirituality but forcefully attempting to abuse the church. Paul also says that these men would "arise from among your own selves" and they would speak "twisted things, to draw away the disciples after them." So then, we see that wolves will also arise from within the church. These kinds of wolves are those Christ warned of in Matthew 7:15, "Beware false prophets, who come to you in sheep's clothing but inwardly are ravenous wolves." The Apostle Peter warned of the same, saying, "But false prophets also arose among the people, just as there will be false teachers among you, who will secretly bring in destructive heresies, even denying the Master who bought them, bringing upon themselves swift destruction" (2 Pet 2:1). The wolves that come from within the church put on a pretense of spirituality, but their appetites for gain and their vicious disregard for the sheep is the same as the wolves that come from the outside. These wolves do not typically devour in plain sight as do those spoken of in verse 28, but they instead *lure* the sheep away with false teaching and smooth talk. Shepherds must be alert for both kinds of wolves and must be ready to extinguish the threat before any harm can come to the sheep.

While wolves take no consideration of the value of the flock, we see here in Paul's charge that the church consists of those whom Jesus "obtained with His own blood." Christ "obtained," "*periepoiēsato*," that is acquired possession with considerable effort. We recall here the purchase price of the church: the incalculably precious death of the Lord Jesus. Peter speaks of the cost in this way, "You were ransomed from the futile ways inherited from your forefathers, not with perishable things such as silver or gold, but with the precious blood of Christ, like that of a lamb without blemish or spot" (1 Pet 1:18–19). While wolves concern themselves only with what they can get from the sheep, we must remember that the people of God were not purchased *by* us or *for* us; Jesus purchased the church, and she exists for His glory alone. God has made the shepherds of the local church to be stewards of His precious people until the day He receives them unto Himself and takes an accounting of the vigilance of the shepherds. So then, as Paul said, we must "be alert," "*grēgoreite*," remaining awake and watchful over the Lord's people.

Again in verse 31, Paul issues the same imperative, "Therefore, be alert." That is, on account of the unceasing presence of danger to the flock, danger from without and within, the elders must remain vigilant. Paul then puts forward his own ministry with the Ephesians as an example of the needed vigilance. He shows by his example that he understood the value of the flock and understood the need for vigilance in caring for them. For "three years" Paul notes that he "did not cease night or day to admonish every one with tears." There was never a time in his three-year ministry in Ephesus that Paul let his guard down. He "did not cease," "*ouk epausamēn*," or make an end to his activity of admonishing, "*nouthetōn*" the Ephesian church. To admonish is to provide instruction as to correct behavior and belief, carrying the idea of warning and exhortation. Paul occupied himself by warning the flock to beware of the dangers of false doctrine and the false teachers who spread it. He prepared the Ephesian believers to combat the lies of wolves with truth. With great passion [with "tears"!], he pleaded and exhorted the flock to remain true and faithful to the Lord Jesus. So also, pastors today must be unceasingly vigilant in their ministry.

> Ministry Principle: The call to ministry is the call to vigilance—careful watch over your soul and the souls of those whom the Lord Jesus has entrusted to your care. You must take care to guard your integrity, your teaching, and the people of God. Don't get distracted from the task: provide for the people of God by keeping

yourself from sin, consistently feeding the flock sound doctrine, and preventing them from being preyed upon by wolves.

A Portrait of a Vigilant Ministry

At the 1985 Southern Baptist Convention Pastors Conference, W.A. Criswell preached a sermon which proved to be a clarion call for Southern Baptist churches to condemn theological liberalism and fight the good fight of defending the doctrines of the inerrancy and authority of Scripture. His sermon that year, "Whether We Live or Die" in effect drew a line in the sand and called for a verdict, a rallying cry for the Conservative Resurgence. So also, in 1988, at the annual meeting of the Southern Baptist Convention, W.A. Criswell preached another pivotal sermon entitled, "The Curse of Liberalism." Being a witness of the decline of biblical Christianity in America and the destruction of Christian seminaries in the north, Criswell, on a national stage, lambasted the encroachment of theological liberalism and sounded the alarm for Southern Baptists. His vigilance, among many others unnamed here, was marked by a willingness to sound the alarm when danger was identified. Criswell's vigilance is on full display early on in 1973 when he issued this call to Southern Baptists:

> If our preachers, evangelists, pastors, churches, and institutions are true to that expression of faith, we shall live. If we repudiate it, we shall die. God will remove our lampstand out of its place, and we shall no longer continue to be a lighthouse in a stormy sea. As theological liberalism that denies the Word of God has destroyed other churches, the same theological liberalism will destroy us. There is no exception to this judgment whether in individual congregations or denominational associations. Like many others we can continue to exist, having a form of godliness and denying the power thereof, but we shall be dead, spiritually dead, evangelistically dead. Our witness in power and saving grace shall have ceased. Which way shall we go? There is no common ground between infidelity and Christianity.[3]

---

3. Criswell, *Why I Preach that the Bible is Literally True*, 219.

Pay Careful Attention to Yourself

As we observe the Lord Jesus, we see clearly why it is necessary for a minister to pay careful attention to himself. To be sure, Christ never failed nor sinned, but we see in His suffering what happens to the sheep when the shepherd is struck. Jesus forewarned His disciples of this on the night of His betrayal, "You will all fall away because of Me this night. For it is written, 'I will strike the shepherd, and the sheep of the flock will be scattered'" (Matt 26:31). In a similar manner, the calamity of a pastor's fall will always affect the people he has been shepherding. If a minister is not careful to watch over himself and his teaching, the failure of his integrity and/or the failure of his teaching will result in the scattering and spiritual harm of the Lord's people.

Jesus taught a parable in Matthew 24 contrasting the wise servant who remains vigilant and faithful to carry out his ministry to the Lord versus the foolish servant who behaves lawlessly, unalert and unwary for the coming of his master. Read the words of our Lord in Matthew 24:45–51:

> Who then is the faithful and wise servant, whom his master has set over his household, to give them their food at the proper time? Blessed is that servant whom his master will find so doing when he comes. Truly, I say to you, he will set him over all his possessions. But if that wicked servant says to himself, 'My master is delayed,' and begins to beat his fellow servants and eats and drinks with drunkards, the master of that servant will come on a day when he does not expect him and at an hour he does not know and will cut him in pieces and put him with the hypocrites. In that place there will be weeping and gnashing of teeth.

Vigilant ministry is conducted by pastors who know the value of the flock and truly believe that they will be held accountable for the diligence they show in their care. To care for the flock of God, I want to put before you three focal points to fixate the vigilance of your ministry on: your soul, your teaching, and God's people.

Keeping Watch Over Your Soul

As I pointed out earlier, elders must keep watch over their own soul, just as Paul commanded, "Pay careful attention to yourselves" (Acts 20:28). We must guard ourselves against self-destruction by moral failure or any failure of integrity. The key to achieving this is the fear of the Lord. We must remember that we are "those who will give an account" (Heb 13:7, Ezek 34:10). The failure of an elder not only affects his family, but also the flock of God. Tremendous collateral damage is produced by the failure of a pastor. Spiritually immature Christians often struggle because of a pastor's failure, and people who have yet to come to faith are given a reason to walk away. We must also note the great damage which is brought about in a pastor's family: the brokenness and humiliation of his wife and the devastation brought about on the children. Brothers, the cost is exceedingly high, and the dangers are abundant, we cannot afford for a moment to let our guard down. "Therefore let anyone who thinks that he stands take heed lest he fall" (1 Cor 10:12).

Keeping Watch Over Your Teaching

We see the paramount importance of the teaching ministry of a pastor by the emphatic exhortation which Paul issues to Timothy in 2 Timothy 4:1–2, "I charge you in the presence of God and of Christ Jesus, who is to judge the living and the dead, and by His appearing and His kingdom: preach the word; be ready in season and out of season; reprove, rebuke, and exhort, with complete patience and teaching." Our ministry is a work of teaching and preaching for the benefit of the people of God and for the glory of God. The people of God need faithful preaching as it is a vital component of God's design for their spiritual growth. Preaching and teaching can also be highly detrimental to the spiritual well-being of a Christian when that teaching is not doctrinally sound. Recall Paul's command to Timothy, "Keep a close watch on yourself and on the teaching. Persist in this, for by so doing you will save both yourself and your hearers" (1 Tim 4:16). Faithful teaching helps and saves God's people, but unfaithful teaching harms them. Therefore, Paul commands Timothy to guard and carefully watch his teaching.

Doctrinally sound teaching is a critical component of God's design for His church. The importance of teaching is seen in the fact that teachers will receive harsher judgment from God. The Apostle James writes, "Not many of you should become teachers, my brothers, for you know that we who teach will be judged with greater strictness" (Jas 3:1). A vigilant ministry will be marked by careful teaching. We must take every precaution to ensure our teaching is sound, lest we find ourselves fitting the description of false teachers which Paul gives in 1 Timothy 1:6–7, "Certain persons, by swerving from these, have wandered away into vain discussion, desiring to be teachers of the law, without understanding either what they are saying or the things about which they make confident assertions." We must guard our teaching against erroneous interpretation or application and against intentional mishandling or misrepresentation due to the pressures of a godless world. Paul warns of this also by writing, "For the time is coming when people will not endure sound teaching, but having itching ears they will accumulate for themselves teachers to suit their own passions, and will turn away from listening to the truth and wander off into myths" (2 Tim 4:3–4). You must remain vigilant to " . . . guard the deposit entrusted to you. Avoid the irreverent babble and contradictions of what is falsely called "knowledge," for by professing it some have swerved from the faith" (1 Tim 6:20–21). Pastor, "Do your best to present yourself to God as one approved, a worker who has no need to be ashamed, rightly handling the Word of Truth" (2 Tim 2:15).

Protecting God's People

A vigilant ministry is also marked by the protection of God's people from wolves and false teachers. Paul warns the Ephesian elders of the certainty of wolves coming into the church as he tells them, "I know that after my departure fierce wolves will come in among you" therefore the elders are to be "alert" (Acts 20:29,31). It is the responsibility of the elders in a local church to guard the flock from wolves. Surely the command, "be alert" is not intended to be all that Paul is demanding. He is demanding the elders remain alert *so that* they may act decisively when the time comes. Elders must call out false teachers and wolves, identifying their person by name and their error in public. If the pastors of the church do not say something and call them out, who will? It is part of the teaching ministry to instruct God's people *who* to beware of and *what* destructive teachings are spreading.

The Apostle John instructs us on how to handle false teachers when he writes, "If anyone comes to you and does not bring this teaching, do not receive him into your house or give him greeting, for whoever greets him takes part in his wicked works" (2 John 10–11). False teachers are to be identified, rebuked, and refused fellowship with the church until they repent of their wickedness. This treatment is for the good of God's people and is designed to provide opportunity for repentance by the ones walking in falsehood. Paul points this out in the case of Hymenaeus and Alexander, two men who had "made shipwreck of their faith" and whom he "handed

A Vigilant Ministry

over to Satan that they may learn not to blaspheme" (1 Tim 1:19–20). The desired outcome of this discipline of false teachers is the same as the discipline of the adulterous man in Corinth, whom Paul commanded the church at Corinth, "Deliver this man to Satan for the destruction of the flesh, so that his spirit may be saved in the day of the Lord" (1 Cor 5:5).

> Proverbs 4:23 "Keep your heart with all vigilance, for from it flow the springs of life."
>
> Prayer Point: Lord, give *me* the grace to guard *my* heart and in doing so, guard the ministry which You have entrusted to *me*. May You make *me* a faithful watchman over Your precious people, to guard them from wolves and false teachers. Give *me* courage to take action to preserve the purity of teaching and the safety of Your church.

Chapter 10

A Dependent Ministry

"The reason why the Bible spends so much of its time reiterating that God is a strong rock, a firm defense, and a sure refuge and help for the weak, is that God spends so much of His time bringing home to us that we are weak, both mentally and morally, and dare not trust ourselves to find, or to follow, the right road."

— J.I. PACKER[1] —

Acts 20:32 "And now I commend you to God and to the Word of His grace, which is able to build you up and to give you the inheritance among all those who are sanctified."

Commentary

As the Apostle Paul brings a close to his exhortation of the Ephesian elders, he recognizes that his contribution to their growth and maturity has come to an end. He sees no disadvantage in this, and, in fact, points with great confidence to the One who, by His Word, builds, strengthens, and preserves all His people unto the end. He says, "I commend," "*paratithemai*," which means, "to entrust to the care of someone." Paul knows that God is the One who will guard these Ephesian elders, and this should instill great peace and confidence in these men even as their faithful leader departs. Paul not

---

1. Packer, *Knowing God*, 250.

only indicates the One to whom the elders are entrusted, but also the means by which God will build up and preserve these men, namely, "to the Word of His grace." It is by the Word of God that all believers are sanctified and preserved, just as the Lord Jesus prayed in John 17:17, "Sanctify them in the truth; Your Word is truth." Likewise, it was Paul's practice *to entrust* to the Lord the elders in every church, as we read in Acts 14:23, "And when they had appointed elders for them in every church, with prayer and fasting they committed them to the Lord in whom they had believed."

Notice also how Paul points out that "the Word of His grace" is able to "build up," "*oikodomēsai*," which speaks literally of constructing a building, and, when used figuratively, refers to strengthening and making one more able. The Ephesian elders would be put to the test in the face of the coming wolves, especially without the Apostle Paul there any longer. However, the very Word of God that brought these men to saving faith in Christ is the same Word that will fortify them and make them able to stand in the evil day.

Not only will the Word of grace "build up," it will also "give . . . the inheritance among all those who are sanctified" (v. 32). It is the Word of God which ensures for every believer the inheritance of the saints, for the Word of God contains the legal and binding promises of God. Paul has full confidence that the Word of God will preserve the Ephesians to receive their inheritance. The Apostle Peter also spoke of the work of God in protecting and preserving God's people and their inheritance. In 1 Peter 1:3–5 we read:

> Blessed be the God and Father of our Lord Jesus Christ! According to His great mercy, He has caused us to be born again to a living hope through the resurrection of Jesus Christ from the dead, to an inheritance that is imperishable, undefiled, and unfading, kept in heaven for you, who by God's power are being guarded through faith, for a salvation ready to be revealed in the last time.

That Paul would commend these elders to the care of the Lord surely encouraged them, knowing the Lord would continue to work within them to build and preserve them. Without such provision from God, no one could endure. Take heart from the Word of God, as you read these encouraging words, penned by the Apostle Paul in 2 Timothy 1:8–12, concerning his ability to suffer and endure hardship with complete confidence in the Lord's ability and commitment to preserve him:

Therefore do not be ashamed of the testimony about our Lord, nor of me His prisoner, but share in suffering for the gospel by the power of God, who saved us and called us to a holy calling, not because of our works but because of His own purpose and grace, which He gave us in Christ Jesus before the ages began, and which has now been manifested through the appearing of our Savior Christ Jesus, who abolished death and brought life and immortality to light through the gospel, for which I was appointed a preacher and apostle and teacher, which is why I suffer as I do. But I am not ashamed, for I know whom I have believed, and I am convinced that He is able to guard until that day what has been entrusted to me.

Ministry Principle: No man God calls to His ministry is expected to be the source of his own strength or the cause of enduring preservation. The call to ministry is the call to dependency. We can take rest in the truth that we are to be dependent on the care of God to provide for us and preserve us. We can find great comfort in knowing that it is by the Word of God that we will be built up and preserved and it is by the Word of God that our inheritance among the saints is insured.

A Portrait of a Dependent Ministry

We would do well to reflect on the ways in which our predecessors exemplified dependency on the Lord through the hardships and sufferings they endured for Christ. Felix Manz, the Swiss Anabaptist, became the first Anabaptist martyr put to death by Protestants. Convinced that true baptism is only carried out when a person has expressed faith in Christ, Manz was a prominent and well-known preacher in his time. Manz was unsatisfied with the continuation of the unbiblical practice of infant baptism amongst many of the Reformers and pushed back with the truth of Scripture as it pertains to believer's baptism. Manz was undeterred by threats against his person and continued to preach and go house to house proclaiming the truth. After the death of his contemporary, Anabaptist preacher Conrad Grebel, Felix Manz was the most prominent of the Anabaptists, which put him in the crosshairs for persecution. In those days there was a decree from the Swiss government that Anabaptists be executed by *rebaptizing* (drowning). When Manz was sentenced to rebaptism in January 1527, it is said that he preached the gospel to the crowds as he passed by on the road to the

A Dependent Ministry

river. As he was bound by the hands and feet, his cry echoed with dependency on the care of God as he said in Latin, "*In manus tuas, Domine, commendo spiritum meum*" or, "Into Your hands, Lord, I commit my spirit,"[2] saying almost verbatim the words Christ proclaimed on the cross in Luke 23:46. As Manz was only moments away from being thrown into the water to drown, he verbally expressed his faith that the God who brought him to faith in Christ was able to save his soul from death and bring him safely into His kingdom.

Dependent on the Care of God

In Abraham's most trying moment, his faith in God was displayed. Abraham was put to the test, a test to prove the genuineness of his dependence on God, when the Lord demanded that he sacrifice Isaac, the son of promise (Gen 22). Abraham had received many blessings from God, but faith is not proven by the ability to receive blessings, it is proven by the ability to sacrifice good gifts to obey. It is easy to say, "I've got plenty, I'm believing in God for more." It is not easy to say, "I've got plenty, but I'm going to give it all away because God is all I need." The one who can sincerely make the second statement is the one who has learned to be dependent. God rewards faith fully surrendered, willing to forfeit everything to trust and obey. A dependent ministry is a ministry of faith. Paul knew that the Ephesian elders needed to conduct a ministry of faith, because they, just like all of us, were incapable of fulfilling their responsibilities without the care and provision of God.

Paul exhorted young Timothy unto dependence on the Lord, as he said, "You then, my child, be strengthened by the grace that is in Christ Jesus" (2 Tim 2:1). The Apostle also exemplified a dependent ministry, which he described in Philippians 4:11–13:

> Not that I am speaking of being in need, for I have learned in whatever situation I am to be content. I know how to be brought low, and I know how to abound. In any and every circumstance, I have learned the secret of facing plenty and hunger, abundance and need. I can do all things through Him who strengthens me.

It is important to note here that you don't need to learn how to be dependent, you need to learn that you are already dependent. A prideful man

---

2. Estep, *The Anabaptist Story*, 47.

thinks himself independent and self-sufficient, but if we evaluate ourselves by the truth of Scripture, we must confess that without the care of God we are destitute and hopeless. In humility, we must realize our dependence on God, for just as Paul said, dependence on God is the "secret" to becoming content and abounding in every situation.

Dependent on the Word of God

Paul commended the Ephesian elders to "the word of His grace" for at least the two reasons he enumerated in his prayer. First, his commendation was that the Word of God's grace is able to build them up, which is to say that the Scriptures, the promises of God, will fortify and sustain the elders in their lives of service and ministry. So also, as ministers, we need to remember that we are dependent on the Word of God to build us up and fortify us with strength and vitality. Without the Word of God, we will be nothing. Following Paul's instruction to Timothy, we must continue in the Word of God, knowing that it is what has made us wise unto salvation and it is the very means by which God will make us equipped for every good work. Refresh your reading of Paul's famous commendation of God's Word in 2 Timothy 3:14–17:

> But as for you, continue in what you have learned and have firmly believed, knowing from whom you learned it and how from childhood you have been acquainted with the sacred writings, which are able to make you wise for salvation through faith in Christ Jesus. All Scripture is breathed out by God and profitable for teaching, for reproof, for correction, and for training in righteousness, that the man of God may be complete, equipped for every good work.

Our great hope in this life is the promise of God for resurrection from the dead and the inheritance we will receive in the kingdom of God. This *promise* of God ensures the certainty of our inheritance because God cannot lie. Paul points to this in the opening salutation of his letter to Titus, "In hope of eternal life, which God, who never lies, promised before the ages began and at the proper time manifested in His Word through the preaching with which I have been entrusted by the command of God our Savior" (Titus 1:2–3). The hope of our eternal life was secured and certain "before the ages began" *because* God made the promise to do so. He tells Timothy that God gave us this grace in eternity past, as God "saved us and called us to a holy calling, not because of our works but because of His own purpose and grace, which He gave us in Christ Jesus before the ages began" (2 Tim 1:9). So then, in Acts 20, Paul commends the Ephesians to the "word of His grace," reminding them that their eternal inheritance is secure because of the promise of God. What a marvelous comfort to the Christian and the Christian minister—to know that our labors and the investments of our lives in the kingdom of God will not be in vain. A minister who understands his dependency on God's Word for security will be willing to obey in difficult times and endure suffering as a good soldier of Jesus Christ.

> Psalm 119:89 "Forever, O Lord, Your Word is firmly fixed in the heavens."

> Psalm 119:93 "I will never forget Your precepts, for by them You have given me life."

> Prayer Point: Lord, help *me* remember how You have sustained *me* and always provided for *me*. Please give *me* the incredible peace which comes from being dependent upon You to sustain *me*. According to the mercies purchased for *me* by Christ, I ask that You bless *me* with faith and peace, knowing that You will always provide for *me*. Bless *me* with a hunger for Your Word, as I know You will be faithful to build *me* up and strengthen *me* through it.

Chapter 11

A Content and Hard-working Ministry

"God looketh not ... principally at the external part of the work, but much more to the heart of him that doth it."

— RICHARD BAXTER[1] —

Acts 20:33-35 "I *coveted* no one's silver or gold or apparel. You yourselves know that these *hands ministered to my necessities* and to those who were with me. In all things I have shown you that by *working hard* in this way we must help the weak and remember the words of the Lord Jesus, how he himself said, 'It is *more blessed to give than to receive.*'"

Commentary

As Paul begins to conclude his farewell address to the Ephesian elders, he offers himself again as he did in verses 18-21 as an example to emulate, particularly his association and attitude toward material possessions. He plainly says in verse 33, "I *coveted no one's* silver or gold or apparel." It would be easy for Paul to look around and see other's prosperity and wonder why God had not allowed him the same advantage. It is not as if he had never felt the tug of that temptation, for he says "if it had not been for the law, I would not have known sin. For I would not have known what it is

---

1. Baxter, *Practical Works of Richard Baxter*, 111.

A Content and Hard-working Ministry

to covet if the law had not said, *"You shall not covet"* (Rom 7:7). Paul supported himself through bi-vocational means both in Corinth (Acts 18:3; 1 Cor 4:12; 9:12; 15; 2 Cor 11:7; 12:13) and Thessalonica (1 Thess 2:9; 2 Thess 3:7–8). The love of money neither characterized Paul's ministry outwardly (1 Tim 6:5), nor served as sinful inward motivations unbeknownst to others (1 Thess 2:5). In fact, the characterizations he would shun would be one of the very things that would make false teachers manifest themselves (Isa 56:11; Jer 6:13; 8:10; Mic 3:11; 1 Tim 6:5–10; Titus 1:11; 2 Pet 2:3). John Phillips has rightly concluded that Paul would have felt that the man of God "must look above and beyond the wealth of a wealthy man to the wealth of a wealthy God who has promised to supply all we need according to His riches in glory."[2]

Paul did what he had to do to faithfully provide a living for himself and his gospel partners, "You yourselves know that *these hands ministered* to my necessities and to those who were with me" (Acts 20:34). One can also translate "worked" or *"hypēretēsan"* as *served* or *ministered* for Paul truly saw his vocation as part of his ministry. Indeed, this provided an example for others to follow (1 Thess 4:11; 2 Thess 3:9). While Paul had every right to earn a living from the gospel (1 Cor 9:13–15), he did accept support from others (2 Cor 11:7–9; Phil 4:10–19), but most often subsidized his ministry through his own labors so he would be able "in my preaching I may present the gospel free of charge" (1 Cor 9:18). Likely, Paul participated in manual labor ("these hands ministered") either in the early mornings or evenings.[3] His traditional Jewish rearing placed within him not only the willingness to roll up his sleeves but also apply a secular trade to fund his teaching.[4] Kenneth O. Gangel provides a poignant note, "Would God that modern church leaders, many who live in opulence far exceeding that of their parishioners and constituents, would pay heed to this simple teaching from Miletus. The greed against which Paul warned the Ephesian elders seems to be an assumed trait of many popular figures in the modern church."[5]

Others, especially the weak, were ever on the mind of Paul. It was a significant reason for his *laboring* and in fact, one can translate *"kopiōntas"* as "we toiled to the point of growing weary." His attitude and approach always worked out in generosity toward others. He offers as an exemplar for himself

---

2. Phillips, *Exploring Acts*, 408.
3. Bruce, *Paul, Apostle of the Heart Set Free*, 291.
4. Phillips, *Exploring Acts*, 408–409.
5. Gangel, *HNTC*, vol. 5, Acts, 344.

and others, the words of Jesus, "It is more blessed to give than to receive." While never recorded in the Gospels the closest would approximate Luke 6:38, "give, and it will be given to you. Good measure, pressed down, shaken together, running over, will be put into your lap. For with the measure you use it will be measured back to you."[6] To be sure, Jesus and Paul provide a template for the ministry of giving – giving oneself totally to God, His people, and the ministry of the Word.[7] Paul demonstrated in the Pastoral Epistles that avarice was grounds for ministerial disqualification (1 Tim 3:3; Titus 1:7, 11). John Polhill concludes that "the minister is to be a servant, a giver and not a taker . . . The one who leads the flock of God should focus on the needs of others, be more concerned with giving than acquiring."[8]

> Ministry Principle: the pulpits of today are full of unhappy, dissatisfied, discontented fellows always looking for the next big thing. The call to ministry and the call to work hard are not mutually exclusive, they go hand in hand. The ministry that we need today is a *content and hard-working* ministry.

A Portrait of a Content and Hardworking Ministry

There is nothing inherently wrong with ministers seeking to better themselves either denominationally or financially, climbing the ladder of success or looking for wider spheres of influence. Neither is it wrong for a minister to not seek that course – such is the will of God in the life of a man. With either course the goal ought to be the same – to be *content* in the Lord's work and to *labor hard* for Him. Until recently I (Tony) had never heard of John Fawcett (1740–1817). Let me introduce you to him. A contemporary of Andrew Fuller, William Carey and John Newton, the 16-year-old Fawcett found Christ when George Whitefield, the *Marvel of the Age* came through Bradford in 1755 and preached in an open field to 20,000 people from John

---

6. Gangel sees these as deriving from a collection of proverbial sayings either written or oral. Gangel, *HNTC*, vol. 5, *Acts*, 348–349. John Phillips views this statement as common community knowledge akin to John 21:25, "And there are also many other things that Jesus did, which, if every one of them were written down, I suppose not even the world itself could contain the books that would be written." Phillips, *Exploring Acts*, 409. Finally, Richard N. Longenecker perceives this as a post ascension revelatory oracle. Longenecker, *EBC*, vol. 9, *Acts*, 514.

7. Hughes, *Acts: The Church Afire*, 280.

8. Polhill, *NAC*, *Acts*, 429–430.

3:14. Fawcett recounted, "As long as life remains, I shall remember both the text and the sermon."[9] Three years later, Fawcett became a Baptist and in 1760 he pursued the call to ministry and preached his first public sermon in 1763.

His first preaching experience outside his home church was at the Baptist church in Wainsgate on December 18, 1763, and he preached there every other week until May 1764 when he began to be a regular weekly fixture. In July of the next year, he received a unanimous vote. Fawcett describes beginning the *hard-working* ministry there at Wainsgate and Albert Bailey provides detail of just how challenging a task he faced:

> I have now set my hand to the plough, and have made a solemn entrance upon the work of the ministry. My partner in life and I have taken leave of our dear friends and brethren, with whom we had an affectionate and sorrowful parting. I would now apply with diligence to the work incumbent upon me. I am conscious of great weakness and inability; but the language of my heart is, 'Lord help me!'[10]
>
> The people were all farmers and shepherds, poor as Job's turkey; an uncouth lot whose speech one could hardly understand, unable to read or write; most of them pagans cursed with vice and ignorance and wild tempers. The Established Church had never touched them; only the humble Baptists had sent an itinerant preacher there and he had made a good beginning.[11]

By 1769 the rural church was alive and thriving and his status and notoriety grew; so much so that Carter Lane Baptist Church in London asked him to fill in for the ailing John Gill. On Gill's passing, Fawcett was Carter Lane's choice and Fawcett gave every indication he would accept. Even though Wainsgate flourished spiritually and numerically, they were a poor church and could ill afford to compensate Fawcett like the prestigious London church. As he and his wife prepared to leave their church *in the wilderness*, their love for the flock compelled them to remain, "His attachment to them was so deeply fixed, that he concluded, at once, to cast himself upon Providence, and live and die with them."[12] Fawcett forfeited the prestigious Gill pulpit and remained with his beloved flock. He did not

---

9. Fawcett, *Account of the Life*, 16.
10. Fawcett, *Account of the Life*, 111.
11. Bailey, *Gospel in Hymns*, 136.
12. Fawcett, *Account of the Life*, 174.

live in a parsonage and his salary was a paltry £25 pounds ($200) a year for a family of 6. The church supplemented his meager stipend with wool and potatoes. Fawcett ended up being their pastor for a total of 54 years. When King George III, an admirer, offered to help, Fawcett, being a Nonconformist, responded, "I have lived among my own people, enjoying their love. God has blessed my labors among them, and I need nothing which even a king could supply."[13]

His near exodus for Carter Lane served as the inspiration behind one of Fawcett's most beloved hymns, "Blest Be the Tie that Binds." The following are the first and fourth stanza:

> Blest be the tie that binds
> Our hearts in Christian love;
> The fellowship of kindred minds
> Is like to that above.
> When we asunder part,
> it gives us inward pain;
> but we shall still be join'd in heart,
> and hope to meet again.

Fawcett was a prolific writer of 165 other hymns, various essays, pamphlets, and books. In 1777, Fawcett built a new chapel at nearby Hebden Bridge and began a ministry academy for pastors. Fawcett developed a school for the area children by adding on to his home. In 1793, he received an invitation to become President of the Baptist Academy at Bristol but declined. In 1811, he published a two-volume illustrated family Bible which led Brown University (Providence, RI) to award him a doctorate. His works include:

- *Poetic Essays*, 1767
- *The Christian's Humble Plea, a Poem, in Answer to Dr. Priestley Against the Divinity of Our Lord Jesus Christ*, 1772
- *The Death of Eumenio, a Divine Poem*, 1779
- *The Reign of Death*, 1780 (a poem inspired by the death of a friend)
- *Brotherly Love*
- *Hymns Adapted to the Circumstances of Public Worship and Private Devotion*, 1782

---

13. Bailey, *Gospel in Hymns*, 138.

A Content and Hard-working Ministry

- *Considerations relative to the sending of missionaries to propagate the Gospel among the Heathens* (for Fuller's Baptist Missionary Society)

Certainly, Fawcett's example will not be God's path for every pastor. Indeed, God leads many ministers to new fields of ministry and expanded spheres of influence. Yet, here in relative obscurity he *toiled*, an example of faithfulness and perseverance. Orphaned at 12, he became an indentured servant at 13, worked 14 hours a day, and taught himself to read at night. A *hardworking* ministry with plenty of fruit to show. As the saying goes, "Some people are like blisters, they only show up after the work is over." Not true of the *toilsome* Fawcett, who epitomized the words of Jesus that "No one who puts his hand to the plow and looks back is fit for the kingdom of God" (Luke 9:62). And what a minister's package! He sacrificed the prestigious pulpit (well, there goes denominational influence and affluence), lived on a fixed wage of £25 pounds a year ($200 or the modern equivalent of $6,874.59 – so much for the denomination's compensation plan), had no parsonage or housing allowance (oh my, you usually get one or the other, right?) and had a retirement plan of wool and potatoes (how is that for a stock portfolio?). When King George offered his help, his reply? "I need nothing which even a king could supply," for his King would never fail him and Fawcett knew that "my God will supply every need of yours according to his riches in glory in Christ Jesus" (Phil 4:19). This is the type of ministry we *need*; I am just not sure it is the type some *want*.

Content – Considering God's Provision

Content – the dictionary defines this as "a state of peaceful happiness." A synonym would be "satisfied." When thinking of this in terms of the believer we could say "a state of peaceful happiness with God and His provision." To be sure, God expects each of His children to be content, but how much more to those whom He has made stewards over His ministry? While this text specifically covers contentment with God's financial provision ("I coveted [desired] no one's silver or gold or apparel"), ministerially speaking, it can, and does, cover a wide range of topics. Verses 33–35 provide Paul as the pivotal example of avoiding the pit of greed and covetousness at all costs. Covetousness is one of the chief means as to how the sin of discontentment reveals itself. Covetousness is an attitude, a longing to acquire things. This runs against the grain and in opposition to the belief that, "And my God will supply every need of yours according to his riches in glory in Christ Jesus" (Phil 4:19). The Lord warned of serious pitfalls related to covetousness and materialism, "Take care, and be on your guard against all covetousness, for one's life does not consist in the abundance of his possessions" (Luke 12:15).

Certainly, neither the man doing his best to care for his family nor the negation of "The laborer deserves his wages" (1 Tim 5:18) is in question here – concerning these two areas both common sense and diligence should prevail. Nevertheless, there is always the temptation to focus too much on "that which fadeth away," to compromise our testimonies and forget our integrity for the sake of material gain, but the minister must remember that God wants him to be *content* – "He who loves money will not be satisfied with money, nor he who loves wealth with his income; this also is vanity" (Eccl 5:10). It is a matter of the minister's personal holiness that he finds satisfaction in what God provides, "Keep your life free from love of money, and be content with what you have, for he has said, "I will never leave you nor forsake you" (Heb 13:5). Nonconformist and Puritan stalwart Jeremiah Burroughs states:

> But a child of God has not a right merely by donation; what he has is his own, through the purchase of Christ. Every bit of bread you eat, if you are a godly man or woman, Jesus Christ has bought it for you. You go to market and buy your meat and drink with your money, but know that before you buy it, or pay money, Christ has bought it at the hand of God the Father with his blood. You have it at the hands of men for money, but Christ has bought it at the hand of his Father by his blood. Certainly it is a great deal better and sweeter now, though it is but a little.[14]

Paul's theology on material goods bears testimony throughout his epistles. He never used God's provision as means to obscure greed, "For we never came with words of flattery, as you know, nor with a pretext for greed—God is witness" (1 Thess 2:5). At Corinth, he was self-supporting (Acts 18:3; 1 Cor 4:12; 9:12; 12:13) as well as Thessalonica, "For you remember, brothers, our labor and toil: we worked night and day, that we might not be a burden to any of you, while we proclaimed to you the gospel of God" (1 Thess 2:9; cf. 2 Thess 3:7–8). Verse 34 indicates that they followed suit at Ephesus and encouraged others to imitate his *modus operandi* (1 Thess 4:11; 2 Thess 3:9). Ministers are not exempt from greed and in

---

14. Burroughs, "The Rare Jewel of Christian Contentment," 34.

some quarters, they may be more susceptible. Paul instructed Timothy on trusting in riches instead of God, "As for the rich in this present age, charge them not to be haughty, nor to set their hopes on the uncertainty of riches, but on God, who richly provides us with everything to enjoy" (1 Tim 6:17). He required material contentment as a major qualification for those who minister (Titus 1:11). Stephen and David Olford sound a clarion call, "If preachers do not go astray theologically or morally, they often wreck themselves on the rocks of material gain."[15] The pastor should be above reproach in all his personal finances, "Moreover, he must be well thought of by outsiders, so that he may not fall into disgrace, into a snare of the devil" (1 Tim 3:7) – people are watching from without and from within. Therefore, the preacher should be thankful and *content* with what he receives, faithful in his giving to God, pay his bills on time, and not run up debt, especially in his community. If what he receives is somehow insufficient, there is nothing wrong with being creative and entrepreneurial to supplement his income if it does not interfere with home or ministry.

The minister today needs to be reminded of a problem that is as fresh as the next new thing in modern ministry yet as old as Paul's first warnings to the ancient church. Love of money or covetousness is the trademark and the way of the false teacher as 1 Timothy 6:5–10 affirms:

> and constant friction among people who are depraved in mind and deprived of the truth, imagining that godliness is a means of gain. But godliness with contentment is great gain, for we brought nothing into the world, and we cannot take anything out of the world. But if we have food and clothing, with these we will be content. But those who desire to be rich fall into temptation, into a snare, into many senseless and harmful desires that plunge people into ruin and destruction. For the love of money is a root of all kinds of evils. It is through this craving that some have wandered away from the faith and pierced themselves with many pangs (cf. Isa 56:11; Jer 6:13; 8:10; Mic 3:11; 2 Pet 2:3).

Anything a minister has; he is to hold loosely and *everything* he needs; he understands the Lord supplies. A minister will find himself in a precarious place if he uses his position and calling for personal gain. When the minister begins to look at the people of God – the church, as a cow to milk instead of sheep to feed, then he is a hireling and forfeits his privilege to minister in God's name.

---

15. Olford and Olford, *Anointed Expository Preaching*, 42.

As stated earlier, *contentment* in the ministry is not simply a matter of what the Lord provides materially. There is also the consideration of being *content* with success or lack thereof, ministerial placement, spiritual gifting, influence, standing, etc. When you struggle with being *content* remember:

- Your current ministry is a call from God. Discontentment is often a result of questioning God's call. "Extraordinary calls may come and I pray they may come to some here present, but they are not likely to be given to those who cannot use their present everyday opportunities. We may be called to very special service and have special Grace given, but it is best for us, till such calls are felt, to mind our business in the station of life in which God has placed us."[16]

- Your faithfulness is what counts. God will not base His judgment on ministerial *magnitude*, but on ministerial *faithfulness*, "This is how one should regard us, as servants of Christ and stewards of the mysteries of God. Moreover, it is required of stewards that they be found faithful. But with me it is a very small thing that I should be judged by you or by any human court. In fact, I do not even judge myself. For I am not aware of anything against myself, but I am not thereby acquitted. It is the Lord who judges me" (1 Cor 4:1–4).

- Your *present* people need the gospel as much *potential* people you are imagining. Looking for greener pastures may mean you neglect the pasture you are in.

- Your faithful presentation of the gospel should be joyful whether to the *few* or the *many*.

- Your *current* ministry is preparation for *later* ministry opportunities.

- Your desire for future opportunities may render you ineffective because you lack focus.

Puritan Thomas Watson wrote a 74-page exposition on Philippians 4:11, "Not that I am speaking of being in need, for I have learned in whatever situation I am to be content." He wrote a whole chapter on the *rules about contentment*:

- Rule 1. Advance faith.
- Rule 2. Labour [sic] for assurance.

16. Spurgeon, "Rahab," pt. 2–para. 9.

A Content and Hard-working Ministry

- Rule 3. Get a humble spirit.
- Rule 4. Keep a clear conscience.
- Rule 5. Learn to deny yourselves.
- Rule 6. Get much of heaven into your heart.
- Rule 7. Look not so much on the dark side of your condition, as on the light.
- Rule 8. Consider in what a posture we stand here in the world.
- Rule 9. Let not your hope depend upon these outward things.
- Rule 10. Let us often compare our condition.
  - Comparison 1st. Let us compare our condition and our desert together
  - Comparison 2d. Let us compare our condition with others; and this will make us *content*
  - Comparison 3d. Let us compare our condition with Christ's upon earth
  - Comparison 4th. Let us compare our condition with what it was once
  - Comparison 5th. Let us compare our condition with what it shall be shortly
- Rule 11. Go not to bring your condition to your mind but bring your mind to your condition.
- Rule 12. Study the vanity of the creature.
- Rule 13. Get fancy [extravagance] regulated.
- Rule 14. Consider how little will suffice nature [all you need is bread and water].
- Rule 15. Believe the present condition is best for us.
- Rule 16. Do not too much indulge the flesh.
- Rule 17. Meditate much on the glory which shall be revealed.
- Rule 18. Be much in prayer.[17]

---

17. Watson, "Art of Divine Contentment," ch. 14–use 5.

Are you *content* with what God supplies? Are you *content* with what God supplies even if God's people are stingy? Are you *content* with where God has placed you? Are you *content* with the sheep you have or do you covet the sheep of another pasture?

Hard Working – Considering God's Creative Mandate

God's design for man from the beginning was that he was to work by his own hands. He told them to "Be fruitful and multiply and fill the earth and subdue it" (Gen 1:28). Adam follows the pattern of His Creator, who "rested from all his work that he had done in creation" (Gen 2:3). In this God neither exerted Himself nor exhausted Himself. Therefore, sequentially we know that work is not the result of sin or the Fall. "The Lord God took the man and put him in the garden of Eden to work it and keep it" (Gen 2:15) and He intended him to *labor* and flourish there. All energy exerted, the time and attention put forth, the skill of the laborer would fulfill the Divine mandate of fruitfulness, filling the earth and exercising dominion. In the end we must understand that *to work* is *to be human*. With the onset of sin and God's curse, he also cursed the still necessary work that God proclaimed good:

> Cursed is the ground because of you; in pain you shall eat of it all the days of your life; thorns and thistles it shall bring forth for you; and you shall eat the plants of the field. By the sweat of your face you shall eat bread, till you return to the ground, for out of it you were taken; for you are dust, and to dust you shall return (Gen 3:17–19).

So, it will be until the end of the age when God removes the curse (Rom 8:21), when man can work freely in the kingdom as he once did.

When we think of the biblical mandate to *work* today, it is not simply what we do for a living or the money we might earn to meet our needs. The starting point is always "these hands ministered" (Acts 20:34; cf. 1 Cor 4:12). Paul *worked*, not simply as a spiritual façade to cover up personal sloth, but as an artisanal tentmaker. Regarding *work*, Paul practiced what he preached, putting himself forth as a faithful example of the divine mandate to *work* (1 Thess 2:9; 2 Thess 3:7–8). While it is true Paul sometimes received financial support (2 Cor 11:7–19; Phil 4:10–19), he understood he had the right to make a living from the gospel (1 Cor 9:13–15) and so he could then say "What then is my reward? That in my preaching I may present the gospel free of charge, so as not to make full use of my right in the gospel" (1 Cor 9:18). Paul also understood *work* as the obligation of every man but especially the believer (1 Thess 4:11–12). Laziness, sloth, and mendacity are part of the old man and should fade and experience transformation by the *work* of Christ and the power of the Spirit, "Let the thief no longer steal, but rather let him *labor*, doing honest *work with his own hands*, so that he may have something to share with anyone in need" (Eph 4:28). When Jesus comes into a life the way of ease becomes less common (that is not to deny the wisdom in working smarter, not harder) and the path of least resistance becomes the road less traveled. Instead, many live by the adage, "All honey and no bees, no work and all ease." Certainly, the proper biblical *work* ethic goes beyond the simple 40-hour week, it is a lifestyle, it is a mindset.[18] Paul celebrated this type of work ethic (Rom 16:6, 12; Col 4:13; 2 Tim 2:6) and condemned laziness (1 Thess 5:15; 2 Thess 3:6, 7, 11; Titus 1:12–13) in the tradition of Solomon. To be lazy is to lack godly *righteousness*, "The way of a sluggard is like a hedge of thorns, but the path of the *upright* is a level highway" (Prov 15:19). One will reap what they sow, "The desire of the sluggard kills him, for his hands refuse to labor" (Prov 21:25). *Work* and *working hard* is the divine mandate for all of humanity. How much more for those who have experienced God's completed *work* in a saving way (something humans *do not* have to *work* for)?

Hard Working – Considering God's Holy Calling

For some, ministry is simply a career path. What those *some* fail to realize is that ministry is not simply a career, it is a calling. This type of person perceives the ministry as consisting of short hours and good pay. Besides, the minister, in the end, only preaches 2–3 hours a week, has an occasional hospital visit or funeral. The preacher arrives on Sunday for 30–40 minutes of impromptu "as the Lord leads" to rally the troops. If he does prepare, it is one of numerous sermonic offerings he takes from church to church – what a life! That perception is in fact, not the reality. John MacArthur asserts that, "The ministry may be a heavenly pursuit, but it is also an earthly task

---

18. We are not overlooking the need here for proper biblical rest. Whether we call that rest days off, vacation, sabbatical, getting away or down time, the point is that *rest* is as much a part of the divine mandate as *work*—if a man does not *come apart* for rest, he will *come apart*!

– it's hard work. That's why the Apostle Paul described his daily pastoral activities by saying "we labor and strive" (1 Tim 4:10)."[19]

God expects all men to *work hard*, believers even more so because they have experienced the transforming power of the Spirit. What of those that God has called to the ministry? Since that man ought to be blameless, since certain truths should characterize and qualify him, his *work* for the Lord should be on a scale *par excellence* and above reproach. Ministry is not for the lazy for it demands *work* that is *hard and toilsome*, it requires sweat and in some cases blood. Paul illustrated work analogous to this by employing the soldier, the athlete, and the farmer (2 Tim 2:1–14). The soldier faithfully works to maintain a singular goal of obeying his superior; the athlete works within parameters so that they might win a crown; and the hardworking farmer exerts himself so that he may enjoy a bountiful harvest. In each of these, discipline is a requirement.

By no means was Paul the first to speak about the *work* of the ministry. Jesus described working in the spiritual field of the Lord and He informed His disciples that "The harvest is plentiful, but the laborers are few. Therefore pray earnestly to the Lord of the harvest to send out laborers into his harvest" (Luke 10:2; cf. Matt 9:37–38). Neither Jesus or Paul begrudged compensation for ministry work – "for the laborer deserves his food" (Matt 10:10); "for the laborer deserves his wages" (Luke 10:7); and "For the Scripture says, "You shall not muzzle an ox when it treads out the grain," and, "The laborer deserves his wages" (1 Tim 5:18). Still, Paul viewed ministry as *labor* and his concern about his ministry being useless and empty had little to do with how he supplemented his income – "be steadfast, immovable, always abounding in the *work* of the Lord, knowing that in the Lord your *labor* is not in vain" (1 Cor 15:58); Galatians 4:11 "I am afraid I may have *labored* over you in vain" (Gal 4:11); "So that in the day of Christ I may be proud that I did not run in vain or *labor* in vain" (Phil 2:16); and "I sent to learn about your faith, for fear that somehow the tempter had tempted you and our *labor* would be in vain" (1 Thess 3:5). Frequently Paul refers to those who *labor* with him as fellow "workers," "prisoners," "soldiers," and "servants."

Working hard for the sake of *working hard* misses the point. We do the work of the ministry because we love God and we love others, and everything in ministry is "*work heartily*, as for the Lord and not for men" (Col 3:23). When speaking of the minister's work, Paul said it should be "your work of

---

19. MacArthur, "Servant Leader Works Hard," para. 2.

A Content and Hard-working Ministry

faith and *labor* of love" (1 Thess 1:3). This type of ministerial work ethic caused Paul to declare "For this I *toil, struggling* with all his energy that he powerfully works within me" (Col 1:29) and "for to this end we *toil* and *strive*, because we have our hope set on the living God" (1 Tim 4:10). "Labor" (*kopiōmen*) means "to work to the point of weariness" and "strive" (*agōnizometha*) means "to agonize in a struggle." We labor though weary, and we strive no matter how agonizing because our work is for the Lord and the outcomes are of eternal consequences. Christian preaching and pastoral ministry are *toilsome* and if it is not that type of ministry, then that man is a failure – "Do your best to present yourself to God *as one approved*, a worker who has no need to be ashamed, rightly handling the word of truth" (2 Tim 2:15). Charles Spurgeon describes such a botched and inept ministry:

> I cannot imagine the Spirit waiting at the door of a sluggard, and supplying the deficiencies created by indolence. Sloth in the cause of the Redeemer is a vice for which no excuse can be invented. We ourselves feel our flesh creep when we see the dilatory movements of sluggards, and we may be sure that the active Spirit is equally vexed with those who trifle in the work of the Lord.[20]

Paul recognized the proper balance of God's work in us and our work for Him, "But by the grace of God I am what I am, and his grace toward me was not in vain. On the contrary, I *worked harder* than any of them, though it was not I, but the grace of God that is with me" (1 Cor 15:10). The key for renewed strength to *labor in* the ministry is God's continual *work in us* (Phil 2:12-13; 4:13; Col 1:29; 1 Tim 1:12).

The call to preach is a call to hard work. The minister's calling is a call to *excellence*, and this applies to sermon preparation and delivery. The Scriptures tell us that "those who *labor* in preaching and teaching" (1 Tim 5:17) are worthy of double honor. Gifting for proclamation may vary by degree, but the ground is level at the threshing floor. While certainly there is the overflow effect as one preaches, the man of God is a wordsmith, for he exerts great energy in the words he *says* and the way that he *uses* them, for he knows they are not just *his words*, he is dispensing *His Word* as well (1 Tim 4:16; 2 Tim 2:15). David Mathis speaks to this action:

> Part of what makes pastoring hard work is that we teach with a tether. We don't just sit down with a blank piece of paper, or show up to address an attentive church, and speak off the top of our heads. Unashamed workers "rightly handle the word of truth"

20. Spurgeon, *Lectures to My Students*, 213.

(2 Timothy 2:15). Week after week, day after day, the words we breathe out to feed the church are not our own thoughts on the matter.[21]

There is an inextricable link between the *Word* of God and the *man* of God. For him, it is not simply *a* book among many – it is *the* book, it is not a book that *contains* God's words – it *is* God's Word. It is the sole authority for Christian faith and practice, for that reason the Book is in our *hand*, in our *head* and in our *heart*. Preachers have a heavenly charge for an earthly mission, "I charge you in the presence of God and of Christ Jesus, who is to judge the living and the dead, and by his appearing and his kingdom: *preach the word*; be ready in season and out of season; reprove, rebuke, and exhort, with complete patience and teaching" (2 Tim 4:1–2). We have a charge from God – *Preach the Word* – how can we not work hard? When I was young, I remember people praying for God to hide the preacher "behind the cross." We all knew what that meant, for the preacher to humbly submit himself to the Lord and to only say what He would have him say. For that reason, we may appropriately "hide behind the cross," but we cannot hide behind the pulpit, for the preacher is there, for the world to see. Has he put forth the effort? Has he worked hard with God's Word? Has he battled with words? Is he ready to enter the fight for the faith? Is he ready to preach as he has never preached before? Indeed, the heavenly message is worth a *hard-working* ministry.

If God is not working *in* you as you work *for* him then you have a treadmill ministry – you are running a lot and getting nowhere! Some do not work – *they are lazy*; some work without allowing God to work in them – *they are foolish*. For the minister who has been either, there is hope – "For we are his workmanship, created in Christ Jesus *for good works*, which God prepared beforehand, that we should walk in them" (Eph 2:10). The marks that identify a *hard-working* ministry are blood, sweat, tears, weariness, aches, pains, loneliness, struggle, exertion, discipline, focus, rising early, staying up late, perseverance, and sacrifice. Paul labored because of the eternal consequences of his effort; yes, heaven is eternal – so is hell! J. Oswald Sanders said, "True leadership always exacts a heavy toll on the whole man, and the more effective the leadership is, the higher the price to be paid."[22] Vance Havner sums it up well, "Where are the marks of the

---

21. Mathis, "Plague of Lazy Pastors," para. 9.
22. Sanders, *Spiritual Leadership*, 175.

A Content and Hard-working Ministry

cross in your life? Are there any points of identification with your Lord? Alas, too many Christians wear medals but carry no scars."

Proverbs 12:14 "From the fruit of his mouth a man is satisfied with good, and *the work of a man's hand* comes back to him."

Prayer Point: Lord, may *I* be content with the provision that You give, the place You called *me* to, and the gifts and calling that come from You. May all *my* work be "as unto the Lord" and may the energy *I* exert be for the glory of God. While "every good and perfect gift" comes from You, may *I* find ultimate contentment in You.

Chapter 12

A Relational Ministry

*" . . . being a shepherd does not mean merely
getting the overall picture from a distance;
it requires getting right in among the flock
and leading by example. It is not leadership from
on high so much as leadership from within."*

— JOHN MACARTHUR[1] —

Acts 20:36–38 "And when he had said these things, he knelt down and prayed with them all. And there was much weeping on the part of all; they embraced Paul and kissed him, being sorrowful most of all because of the word he had spoken, that they would not see his face again. And they accompanied him to the ship."

Commentary

The final scene of Paul's farewell to the Ephesians is quite emotional. He has already told the elders that they would not see his face again (v. 25), and while they certainly had hope in the resurrection, the sadness of never seeing or spending time in this age with their beloved Apostle was heartbreaking. Surely, as Paul exhorted the Ephesians to remember the command of the Lord, "It is more blessed to give than to receive," their minds were

---

1. MacArthur, *Pastoral Ministry*, 23.

A Relational Ministry

populated to some degree with the Apostle's example of self-sacrifice and how much they benefited from him giving of himself to them in ministry and fellowship.

That there was "much weeping," indicates a depth of relationship between Paul and the church at Ephesus. The word used here for "weeping" is "*klauthmos*," and refers to weeping or wailing with a particular emphasis on the noise accompanying the lament. This type of cry is an emotional outburst, a weeping which causes one to whimper and moan, even the gasping for air. In addition to the weeping, the Ephesians "embraced" (*epipesontes*) Paul, which means they "fell on his neck" in flinging their arms around him in an embrace of deep affection. Even more, the Ephesians each "kissed" Paul, not as a sign of sensuality, but in an act of special affection and appreciation.

Paul was not merely their Apostle and teacher; he was their friend and their brother. Take note that the lament was shared by "all," that is, there was unity in the affection which Paul and the Ephesians had for one another. Broken hearted as their dear friend was departing, they gathered around him and "accompanied him to the ship," and there is no doubt that the outpouring of emotion continued in that walk and even as the ship sailed off out of sight.

Similarly, after Paul had spent only seven days with the believers in Tyre, all the men, their wives, and their children accompanied Paul to the beach, where all knelt down around him in prayer and bid farewell (Acts 21:5–6). Even in a short stint, Paul made a relational connection with the people, whereby they were assured of his love for them and in turn they reciprocated. So also in Caesarea, the believers became heartbroken at the prophecy of Paul's impending arrest and began with tears pleading with him to not go up to Jerusalem (Acts 21:10–14).

Paul not only had a relational ministry with the churches he had served, he also had a deeply affectionate relationship with the young pastor he mentored. Referring to Timothy as his "beloved" "*agapēton*" child in the faith, we observe Paul's affection for Timothy as that of a father to his son (1 Tim 1:2, Rom 16:21, 1 Cor 4:17, Phil 2:22). Timothy shared such affection for Paul as well, marked by his "tears," which likely refers to an emotional farewell earlier on in his life when the Apostle continued and left the young pastor behind until a later date. Amongst both the congregation of the churches and the ministers he mentored, Paul exemplified a relational ministry.

Ministry Principle: Large congregations, big buildings, huge budgets, name recognition, and much more tempt pastors to view the people they serve as an opportunity for self-advancement. Such a mindset is not only carnal, it is abhorrent to God and produces wolves who seek to devour rather than shepherds ready to serve. The call to ministry is the call to love, to sacrifice, and to serve. God has not called us to loveless ministry. The ministry that we need today is a *relational* ministry.

A Portrait of a Relational Ministry

I (Jordan) know a pastor who truly exemplifies a *relational* ministry, we can call him Bro. Jim. I never knew a single person in the church he served who testified that they doubted Jim's love and care for them. When church members went through a crisis, he never failed to reach out to them to express his sympathy and to offer help. When someone had a joyful experience, Jim always shared their joy and was delighted to see them succeed and be glad. I watched him minister to families in the hospital and at funeral visitations, never failing to share Jesus and express his own love and compassion. I watched members of the church take great comfort from just a simple word of prayer or a gentle hug from Bro. Jim.

I have come to understand through the years that there are many pastoral shortcomings a church congregation will be gracious about, but one they will not tolerate is an uncaring and cold pastor. A pastor is, first and foremost, a preacher and teacher of God's Word, but he is not *only* that. A pastor must have a relationship with the people he is ministering to. Just like Jim, a pastor must share in the joys and trials of the members of the church. He must minister *in their midst*, not just from a distant pulpit. The ministry of a pastor extends far beyond the pulpit and the doors of the church. The ministry of the pastor must extend into the lives of the church members. This is precisely the way in which Calvin described pastoral work:

> ... Christ did not ordain pastors on the principle that they only teach the Church in a general way on the public platform, but that they also care for the individual sheep, bring back the wandering and scattered to the fold, bind up those broken and crippled (*luxatas*), heal the sick, support the frail and weak (Ezek.34:2, 4); for general teaching will often have a cold reception, unless it is helped by advice given in private. Accordingly, there is no excuse for the negligence of those who, after holding one meeting, live for

the rest of the time free from care, as if they have discharged their duty. It is as if their voices were shut up in the sanctuary, since they become completely dumb as soon as they come out of it.[2]

Marks of a Relational Ministry: Affection

A *relational ministry* is marked by affection. That is, you have to love the people. The Apostle Paul provides us with the necessary perspective we must attain if we are to cultivate true affection for the people to whom we minister. Paul employed two metaphors in 1 Thessalonians 2 which describe the perspective of his affection for the Thessalonians. In 1 Thessalonians 2:7, he wrote, "But we were gentle among you, like a nursing mother taking care of her own children."

In this first simile, where he emphasized the gentleness of their conduct before the Thessalonians, he compared his care for them to that of a nursing mother caring for *her own children*. The second metaphor Paul uses is in 1 Thessalonians 2:11–12, where he wrote, "For you know how, like a father with his children, we exhorted each one of you and encouraged you and charged you to walk in a manner worthy of God, who calls you into His own kingdom and glory." So then, their care for the Thessalonians was like a nursing mother to her child and their instruction was like that of a father to his children. Both in his care for the Thessalonians and his instruction, he viewed himself as a parent of the people. Paul also made such a comparison with the Galatians, "my little children, for whom I am again in the anguish of childbirth until Christ is formed in you!" (Gal 4:19). Now, this does not necessitate that Paul was older than all the members of the church, nor does it in any way imply a domineering tone or approach, but it does clearly express his deep affection for the people of God.

Paul's perspective is especially important for all pastors to adopt, and this is why: As a parent, you don't love your children *because* they obey you or *because* they do everything correctly. You don't love your children *because* they behave in perfect maturity or because they are sinless. As a parent, you love your children because they are your children, and God has given you a unique responsibility and stewardship of those children He has entrusted to you. The nursing mother does not discard the infant because of their cries or immaturity, nor does a loving father abuse his children when

---

2. Calvin, *CNTC: The Acts of the Apostles*, 2:175.

they fail to perfectly understand or to carry out his instruction. So also, if you are to develop a *relational ministry* and truly cultivate affection for God's people, you must come to understand that God has entrusted those people to you *so that you will lead them to maturity and spiritual adulthood*! So many pastors whine and complain that their church members are immature and behave in spiritual immaturity, but could that be because their spiritual parents (their pastors) are not truly loving, discipling, and leading the people to spiritual maturity? Children turn into adults not because of physical maturity—there are many adult-bodied adolescents! Children transform into adults because they are taught and disciplined into maturity by those to whom they are entrusted. So then, each pastor must come to see himself rightly, as spiritual mentor and parent to those people whom God has sent him.

Marks of a Relational Ministry: Investment

A *relational ministry* is not only marked by affection but also by investment. Paul was committed not only to preach the gospel to the people, but he was also committed to *share of his own self*. In 1 Thessalonians 2:8, Paul wrote, "So, being affectionately desirous of you, we were ready to share with you not only the gospel of God but also our own selves, because you had become very dear to us." Paul's love for the Thessalonians compelled him to share his own "*psychas*," or "soul" with them. That is, Paul was genuinely pouring out his heart to the Thessalonians, not only giving them the gospel in ministry, but actually being part of the people. In order to have a relational ministry, you are going to have to be part of the church.

Pastor, you can't just show up and preach and minister, you actually need to be involved in the life of the local church. You need to share the people's joys and sorrows, just as Paul instructed in Romans 12:15, "Rejoice with those who rejoice, weep with those who weep." Christians should share together in the highs and lows of life, as a family would. *Together* is the way in which a family experiences joys and sorrows. When we share in life's joys and sorrows, we are investing ourselves emotionally and relationally, thus fulfilling Paul's command in Romans 12:10, "Love one another with brotherly affection."

Many pastors have been hurt deeply in the churches where they have served. For this reason, most pastors are tempted to *not* invest themselves emotionally or relationally in the life of the church. They are content to preach, perform weddings and funerals, and maintain the machinery of the church, but they refuse to truly invest their affections in the people for fear of getting burned again. But we must remember Christ, who though He never sinned, prayed for those who tormented and crucified Him, and entrusted Himself totally to God. We read Christ's prayer for His executioners, "Father, forgive them, for they do not know what they are doing" (Luke 24:34) and we see Christ's example and the accompanying exhortation given by Peter who wrote, "To this you were called, because Christ suffered for you, leaving you an example, that you should follow in His steps. "He committed no sin, and no deceit was found in His mouth." When they hurled their insults at him, he did not retaliate; when he suffered, he made no threats. Instead, he entrusted Himself to Him who judges justly" (1 Pet 2:21–23).

Marks of a Relational Ministry: Prayer

In 10 of the 13 letters he penned, the Apostle Paul communicated to the recipients that he was in diligent prayer on their behalf.[3] Again, Paul's ministerial legacy serves as an example for us to imitate. One of the things we discover in prayer is that the more we pray on behalf of a person the more there is born in us a desire to see God's good blessings given to them. The more we pray for people by name, the more our affections for them are stirred.

It is somewhat easy to pray for those in the congregation who are pleasant, helpful, and friendly. It is incredibly difficult to pray on behalf of those who have done things to harm you. But we are not permitted to exclude those who behave as enemies from our prayers. Here, we recall both the command and the example of Christ. By way of command, the Lord Jesus said, "But I say to you, love your enemies and pray for those who persecute you" (Matt 5:44). In His example, while hanging on the cross, Jesus prayed for His tormentors, "Father, forgive them, for they know not what they do" (Luke 23:34). Among many things accomplished in our hearts when we pray for our enemies is the cultivation of love and a desire to see them granted repentance, and in the case of an unregenerate person—even their salvation. Let us not forget that "while we were enemies we were reconciled to God by the death of His Son" (Rom 5:10).

3. Rom 1:10; 1 Cor 1:4; 2 Cor 13:7; Eph 1:16; Phil 1:4; Col 1:3; 1 Thess 1:2; 2 Thess 1:3, 2 Tim 1:3; Phlm 1:4.

Proverbs 27:23–24, "Know well the condition of your flocks, and give attention to your herds, for riches do not last forever; and does a crown endure to all generations?"

Prayer Point: Lord, give *me* a heart of true love and affection for those to whom You have sent *me* to minister. Cultivate within *me* a genuine desire to not only share the gospel but to also share *my* own soul with Your people. Especially when loving people is difficult, help *me* to remember the example of Christ, who did not retaliate in response to insults nor did He make threats when He suffered, but instead entrusted Himself to You.

Conclusion

Put Your Hand to The Plow

*No one who puts his hand to the plow
and looks back is fit for the kingdom of God* (Luke 9:62)
— JESUS CHRIST —

As important as it is for pastors to have the ability and the reservoir to articulate theological and philosophical ideas *about* ministry, they must be able also to faithfully live those out in the church and the world. Relevance is admirable, but fidelity even more.

We are not interested in what the *world* says about pastors and/or preaching – we are however, interested in what *God's Word* says about pastors, the primacy of preaching, and the tasks of ministry. Paul set out not to defend his ministry but to encourage the Ephesian elders to remember his ministry example. Paul was fearless in his gospel proclamation – in his "testifying" of the Word of God. It is the God of the Word we look to please. Pastors exist to shepherd God's people in His churches until Jesus returns (1 Pet 5:1–5). To that end, God tells each and every one of His shepherds to protect His people, feed them, lead them, and care for them. This is our goal and what *The Ministry We Need: Paul's Ancient Farewell – the Pastor's Present Calling* is all about!

We trust this book has helped you in several ways, guiding you to: 1) identify the 12 aspects of ministry from Acts 20:17–38 that typify the ministry we need: *A Consistent Ministry, A Humble Ministry, A Ready Ministry, A Bold Ministry, A Gospel-centered Ministry, A Spirit-led Ministry, A*

Conclusion

Mission-minded Ministry, A Blameless and Complete Ministry, A Vigilant Ministry, A Dependent Ministry, A Content and Hardworking Ministry and *A Relational Ministry*, 2) minister in an effective way, discerning what you should change or reinforce, 3) feel both a sense of confidence as you are faithful to the ministry God has given you and a sense of conviction in those areas of ministry where you are lacking, 4) identify your story in the pages of *The Ministry We Need*, discover compelling reasons for a ministry that is biblically accurate, theologically sound, practical, relevant, and God-honoring, 5) find encouragement and inspiration from a wide variety of stories, from living and historical figures who kept, or are keeping, their hand to the plow (Luke 9:62), 6) not just learn about *what* pastors do according to Scripture, but *who* they are or *should* be as well – knowing what you believe shapes your life and how you pastor, 7) receive encouragement to "fulfill your ministry (2 Tim 4:5)" and "see that you fulfill the ministry that you have received in the Lord (Col 4:17)," and 8) find benefit from the preaching and pastoral ministry perspective of three practitioners who have experienced the difficulties, stress, and joys of ministry.

This book concludes with 3 scriptural blessings that the authors are praying for all those who allowed us a moment to speak a word about the Word and *The Ministry We Need*.

> Tony — "Now to Him who is able to protect *you* from stumbling and to make *you* stand in the presence of His glory, without blemish and with great joy, to the only God our Savior, through Jesus Christ our Lord, be glory, majesty, power, and authority before all time, now and forever. Amen" (Jude 24–25).

> Jordan — "To this end we always pray for *you*, that our God may make *you* worthy of His calling and may fulfill every resolve for good and every work of faith by His power, so that the name of our Lord Jesus may be glorified in *you*, and *you* in Him, according to the grace of our God and the Lord Jesus Christ" (2 Thessalonians 1:11–12).

Conclusion

Jeremy — "Now may the God of peace Himself sanctify *you* completely, and may *your* whole spirit and soul and body be kept blameless at the coming of our Lord Jesus Christ. He who calls *you* is faithful; He will surely do it" (1 Thessalonians 5:23–24).

About the Authors

Jeremy A. Rogers is the Lead Pastor of Eastwood Baptist Church in Bowling Green KY. He began preaching when he was 13 years old and has been in ministry for 27 years. He is recipient of numerous preaching and ministry awards, and was named to *Who's Who Among Students in American Universities and Colleges* (2010). He holds the DMin in Expository Preaching (Southeastern Baptist Theological Seminary). He has served in many areas of SBC denominational life including the Executive Board of the Southern Baptist of Texas Convention and has served as Adjunct Professor of Preaching at Criswell College. He has book reviews in *Midwestern Journal of Theology* and *Criswell Theological Review*. Jeremy's helpmate and greatest earthly blessing is the former LouAnn Donathan, and they are the parents of Jeremiah (17), SaraBeth (15), EllaGrace (13), Micah (12) and Katerina Joy (10).

Jordan N. Rogers is the Senior Pastor of Hillcrest Baptist Church in Nederland TX. He has pastored for the last 10 years and has been in ministry for 16 years. Jordan played college baseball at San Jacinto JUCO and Rice University. He was drafted to play Major League Baseball by the Colorado Rockies, San Diego Padres, and Chicago Cubs. He holds the PhD in Biblical Studies [emphasis Expository Preaching] (Midwestern Baptist Theological Seminary). He has served in many areas of SBC denominational life including chairman of Southern Baptist of Texas Credentials Committee and as a trustee for Southwestern Baptist Theological Seminary. He is the author of *Authentic Faith: Do I Have Real Faith* (2015), "Proclaim the Glorious Exchange" a contribution in *Evangelism Takes Heart* (2019) and a book review in the *Journal of Biblical and Theological Studies*. Jordan's helpmate and greatest earthly blessing is the former Julia Channing Sallee, and they are the parents of Josiah (12), Elijah (10) and Addie Jo (8).

Tony A. Rogers is the Senior Pastor of Southside Baptist Church in Bowie TX. He has pastored for the last 32 years and has been in ministry for 44 years. He is a member of the Evangelical Theological Society and the Evangelical Homiletics Society. He holds the DMin in Expository Preaching (Midwestern Baptist Theological Seminary). He has served in many areas of SBC denominational life including Chairman of the Board of Criswell College. Book reviews to his credit are in the *Midwestern Journal of Theology, Southwestern Journal of Theology, Criswell Theological Review, Themelios, Journal of Biblical and Theological Studies, Denver Seminary Journal, Southern Baptist Journal of Theology, Scottish Bulletin of Evangelical Theology, Westminster Theological Journal, Studies in Puritanism and Piety Journal*, and *Journal of the Evangelical Homiletics Society*. Tony's helpmate and greatest earthly blessing is the former Terrie Lynn O'Brien and they are the parents of Jeremy (LouAnn), Heather (Robert Blake), and Jordan (Julia). They have 14 grandchildren.

Bibliography

Azurdia, Arturo G., III. *Spirit Empowered Preaching*. Fearn, Ross-shire: Mentor, 1998.
Bailey, Albert. *The Gospel in Hymns: Backgrounds and Interpretations*. New York: Charles Scribner's Sons, 1950.
Barnes, Albert. *Notes on the New Testament: Acts*. Ed. Robert Frew. London: Blackie & Son, 1884–1885.
Barnhouse, Donald Grey. "On Expository Preaching." In *We Prepare and Preach: The Practice of Sermon Construction and Delivery*. Edited by Clarence Stonelynn Roddy, 29–36. Chicago: Moody, 1959.
Bauer, Walter, Frederick W. Danker, W. F. Arndt, and F. W. Gingrich. *A Greek-English Lexicon of the New Testament and Other Early Christian Literature*. Chicago: University of Chicago Press, 2000.
Baxter, Richard. *The Reformed Pastor*. Grand Rapids: Sovereign Grace, 1971.
Begg, Alistair. "A Good Servant of Christ Jesus." www.truthforlife.org. May 8, 2017. https://www.truthforlife.org/resources/sermon/first-general-session-2017/.
Benzinger, Jon. "The Courageous Example of John Macarthur." *For The Gospel* (blog), August 14, 2020. https://www.forthegospel.org/the-courageous-example-of-john-macarthur/.
Bounds, E. M. *Power through Prayer*. 1962. Rev. ed. Grand Rapids: Zondervan, 1977.
Bruce, F. F. *Paul, Apostle of the Heart Set Free*. American ed. Grand Rapids: Eerdmans, 1977.
Bryant, James W., and Mac Brunson. *The New Guidebook for Pastors*. Nashville: B&H, 2007.
Burroughs, Jeremiah. "The Rare Jewel of Christian Contentment." Preach the Word. Accessed August 21, 2020. https://www.preachtheword.com/bookstore/contentment.pdf.
Calvin, John. *Calvin's New Testament Commentaries: The Acts of the Apostles*. Vol. 2. Grand Rapids: Eerdmans, 2005.
Carson, D. A., and Timothy Keller. *Gospel-Centered Ministry*. Edited by D. A. Carson and Timothy Keller. The Gospel Coalition Booklets. Wheaton: Crossway, 2011.
Challies, Tim. "The Gospel-Centered Everything." Challies.com. March 7, 2013. https://www.challies.com/articles/the-gospel-centered-everything/.
Chambers, Oswald. *Biblical Psychology: A Series of Preliminary Studies*. Cincinnati: God's Revivalist Office, 1914. https://archive.org/details/biblicalpsycholoocham/mode/2up.

Bibliography

Charles, H. B., Jr. *On Pastoring: A Short Guide to Living, Leading, and Ministering as a Pastor*. Chicago: Moody, 2016.

Criswell, W. A., *Why I Preach that the Bible is Literally True*. Nashville: Broadman, 1973.

Eclov, Lee. *Persuasion in Preaching: Preaching Today*. Accessed January 4, 2022. https://www.preachingtoday.com/skills/2016/june/persuasion-in-preaching.html

Earls, Aaron. "Restoration, Return Unclear for Adulterous Pastors, New Survey Finds." Baptist Press. August 11, 2020. https://www.baptistpress.com/resource-library/news/restoration-return-unclear-for-adulterous-pastors-new-survey-finds/.

Enns, Paul P. The Moody Handbook of Theology. Revised, ed. Chicago: Moody, 2014.

Estep, William Roscoe. *The Anabaptist Story: An Introduction to Sixteenth-Century Anabaptism*. 3rd ed. Grand Rapids: Eerdmans, 1996.

Fawcett, John. *An Account of the Life, Ministry, and Writings of the late Rev. John Fawcett, D. D.* London: Baldwin, Craddock, and Joy, 1818.

Gallaty, Robby, and Steven L. Smith. *Preaching for the Rest of Us: Essentials for Text-Driven Preaching*. Nashville: B&H Academic, 2018.

Gangel, Kenneth O. *Holman New Testament Commentary*. Edited by Max Anders. Vol. 5, Acts. Nashville: Holman, 1998.

Getz, Gene A. *The Measure of a Man: Twenty Attributes of a Godly Man*. Ventura: Regal, 2004.

Grudem, Wayne. *Bible Doctrine: Essential Teachings of the Christian Faith*. Edited by Jeff Purswell. Grand Rapids: Zondervan, 1999.

Hailey, Corey. "Christians Need to Be 'Marked for Ministry,' Richards Say." Baptist Press. February 9, 2000. https://www.baptistpress.com/resource-library/news/christians-need-to-be-marked-for-ministry-richards-say/.

Hanbury, Aaron. "Twenty Years and Counting: Mohler Reflects on His Presidency at Southern Seminary." Southern Baptist Theological Seminary (EQUIP). Accessed February 4, 2022. https://equip.sbts.edu/publications/towers/twenty-years-%E2%80%A8and-counting-%E2%80%A8mohler-reflects-on-his-presidency-of-southern-seminary/.

Heisler, Greg. *Spirit-led Preaching: The Holy Spirit's Role in Sermon Preparation and Delivery*. Nashville: B&H, 2007.

Henry, Matthew. *Matthew Henry's Commentary on the Whole Bible: Complete and Unabridged in One Volume*. Peabody: Hendrickson, 1994.

Hinkle, Don. "Southern Baptists of Texas Mark Ongoing Hikes in Churches, Giving." Baptist Press. November 17, 1999. https://www.baptistpress.com/resource-library/news/southern-baptists-of-texas-mark-ongoing-hikes-in-churches-giving/.

Hughes, R. Kent. *Acts: The Church Afire*. ESV ed. Preaching the Word. Wheaton: Crossway, 2014.

———. *Disciplines of a Godly Man*. Rev. ed. Wheaton: Crossway, 2006.

Keller, Timothy. *Center Church: Doing Balanced, Gospel-Centered Ministry in Your City*. Grand Rapids: Zondervan, 2012.

Kocman, Alex. "Be Christ-Centered, Not Just Gospel-Centered." Founders Ministries. March 18, 2019. https://founders.org/2019/03/18/be-christ-centered-not-just-gospel-centered/.

Land, Richard. "Ask Dr. Land: Should Fallen Christian Leaders Be Allowed to Return to Ministry?" The Christian Post. May 8, 2020. https://www.christianpost.com/news/ask-dr-land-should-fallen-christian-leaders-be-allowed-to-return-to-ministry.html.

Larkin, William J. *Acts*. Downers Grove, Illinois: IVP, 1995.

Bibliography

Lloyd-Jones, David Martyn. *Preaching and Preachers,* Ministry Resources Library. Grand Rapids: Zondervan, 1972.

Longenecker, Richard N. *The Expositor's Bible Commentary.* Edited by Frank Gaebelein. Vol. 9, *Acts.* Grand Rapids: Zondervan, 1981.

Louw, Johannes P. and Eugene Albert Nida, *Greek-English Lexicon of the New Testament: Based on Semantic Domains.* New York: United Bible Societies, 1996.

MacArthur, John F., Jr. *The Gospel According to Jesus: What Is Authentic Faith?* rev. & expanded anniversary ed. Grand Rapids: Zondervan, 2008.

———. *One Faithful Life: A Harmony of the Life and Letters of Paul.* Nashville: Thomas Nelson, 2019.

———. *Pastoral Ministry: How to Shepherd Biblically.* Nashville: Nelson Reference & Electronic, 2005.

———. *The Power of Integrity: Building a Life Without Compromise.* Wheaton: Crossway, 1997.

———. "The Servant Leader Works Hard." *GTY Blog,* March 13, 2019. https://www.gty.org/library/blog/B190313/the-servant-leader-works-hard.

———. *Truth Matters: Landmark Chapters from the Teaching Ministry of John Macarthur.* 35th Anniversary Anthology (1969–2004). Nashville: Thomas Nelson, 2004.

MacArthur, John F., Jr., and The Master's Seminary Faculty, eds. *Rediscovering Expository Preaching.* Nashville: Thomas Nelson, 1992.

Martyn, Henry, quoted in J. Oswald Sanders, *Spiritual Maturity.* Chicago: Moody, 1994.

Mathis, David. "The Plague of Lazy Pastors: Real Ministry Requires Hard Work." Desiring God. May 22, 2019. https://www.desiringgod.org/articles/the-plague-of-lazy-pastors.

Mayhue, Richard L. "Introductions, Illustrations, and Conclusions." In *Rediscovering Expository Preaching.* Edited by John F. MacArthur Jr. and The Master's Seminary Faculty, 242–54. Dallas: Word, 1992.

Merida, Tony. *Faithful Preaching: Declaring Scripture with Responsibility, Passion, and Authenticity.* Nashville: B&H, 2009.

Mohler, R. Albert., Jr. *He Is Not Silent: Preaching in a Postmodern World.* Chicago: Moody, 2008.

Moody, William R. *The Life of Dwight L. Moody.* New York: Fleming H. Revell, 1900.

Olford, Stephen F., and David L. Olford. *Anointed Expository Preaching.* Nashville: B&H, 1998.

Owen, John. "Book 1 Chapter 1 General Principles Concerning the Holy Spirit and His Work." In *Pneumatologia: Or, a Discourse Concerning the Holy Spirit Complete.* 1674, edited by Anthony Uyl. Reprint, 26. Ontario: Devoted, 2020.

Packer, J I. *Knowing God.* 20th ed. Downers Grove: InterVarsity, 1993.

Patrick, Tim, and Andrew Reid. *The Whole Counsel of God: Why and How to Preach the Entire Bible.* Wheaton: Crossway, 2020.

Perkins, William. Commentary on Galatians. West Linn, OR: Monergism, 2020. https://www.monergism.com/commentary-galatians-ebook.

Peterson, David G. *The Acts of the Apostles,* The Pillar New Testament Commentary (Grand Rapids: Eerdmans, 2009).

Phillips, John. *Exploring Acts: An Expository Commentary.* Grand Rapids: Kregel, 2001.

Piper, John. *Brothers, We Are Not Professionals: A Plea to Pastors for Radical Ministry.* Nashville: Broadman & Holman, 2002.

Bibliography

———. "A Cause to Live For." www.desiringgod.org. December 28, 1986. https://www.desiringgod.org//messages/a-cause-to-live-for.

———. "Greatness, Humility, Servanthood." www.desiringgod.org. August 30, 2009. https://www.desiringgod.org/messages/greatness-humility-servanthood.

Polhill, John B. *Acts*. The New American Commentary. Vol. 26. Nashville: Broadman, 1992.

Prime, Derek J., and Alistair Begg. *On Being a Pastor: Understanding Our Calling and Work*. Rev. and exp. ed. Chicago: Moody, 2004.

Richard Baxter, *The Practical Works of Richard Baxter, Vol. 1: A Christian Directory*. Ligonier: Soli Deo Gloria Ministries, 1990.

Richards, Jim. "Annual Meeting 2018 (2 Timothy 3:10–17)" (MP4). Sermon, Second Baptist Church, Houston, TX, July 28, 2019.

———. "The Baptist Center for Theology and Ministry." New Orleans Baptist Theological Seminary. June 25, 2007. https://www.nobts.edu/baptist-center-theology/interviews-files/Jim_Richards_Jun_2007.pdf.

———. "Easter: The Essential Resurrection." Baptist Press. April 11, 2017. https://www.baptistpress.com/resource-library/news/easter-the-essential-resurrection/.

———. "Pastor-Church Relations" (MP4). Sermon, East Paris Baptist Church, Paris, TX, July 28, 2019.

———. "Seeking Direction in the Church" (MP4). Sermon, East Paris Baptist Church, Paris, TX, March 10, 2019. https://eastparis.org/content.cfm?id=213&download_id=584

———. "The Church and the Pastor" (MP4). Sermon, East Paris Baptist Church, Paris, TX, August 18, 2019.

———. "What Is the One Thing the Next Generation of Pastors Needs to Remember." Midwestern Baptist Theological Seminary (FTC interview). Accessed February 3, 2022. https://vimeo.com/148529786.

Sanders, J. Oswald. *Spiritual Leadership*. Revised. Chicago: Moody, 1980.

SBTS. "Recovering a Vision: The Presidency of R. Albert Mohler. Jr." Southern Baptist Theological Seminary. October 21, 2013. https://www.youtube.com/watch?v=A1k9HyxLiOY.

———. "XXV: The Enduring Vision of Albert Mohler at Southern Seminary." Southern Baptist Theological Seminary. October 11, 2018. https://www.youtube.com/watch?v=b5vS3dgyams.

Spurgeon, Charles Haddon. "A Gospel Worth Dying For (No. 1734)." www.spurgeongems.org. August 12, 1883. https://www.spurgeongems.org/sermon/chs1734.pdf

———. *Lectures to My Students*. Peabody: Hendrickson, 2010

———. "The Minister's Farewell." Sermon, New Park Street, London, UK, December 11, 1859. https://www.spurgeon.org/resource-library/sermons/the-ministers-farewell/#flipbook/.

———. "A Prayer for the Church Militant." Sermon 768, Surrey Chapel, Blackfriars Rd, London, England, undated. https://www.spurgeongems.org/sermon/chs768.pdf.

———. "Rahab." Sermon 1061, The Metropolitan Tabernacle, London UK, July 21, 1872. https://www.ccel.org/ccel/spurgeon/sermons18.xxxiv.html.

———. "To You." Sermon 2899, The Metropolitan Tabernacle, London, England, July 9, 1876. https://www.spurgeongems.org/sermon/chs2899.pdf.

Staff. "40-Year Criswell Prof Honored." www.baptistpress.com. July 14, 2016. https://www.baptistpress.com/resource-library/news/bp-ledger-july-14-2016/.

Bibliography

Strauch, Alexander. *Biblical Eldership: An Urgent Call to Restore Biblical Church Leadership*. rev. and expanded. ed. Littleton: Lewis and Roth, 1995.

Thornbury, Gregory Alan. *Recovering Classic Evangelicalism: Applying the Wisdom and Vision of Carl F. H. Henry*. Wheaton: Crossway, 2013.

Thomas, Derek W. H. *Acts* (Reformed Expository Commentary). Edited by Richard D. Phillips, Philip Graham Ryken, and Daniel M. Doriani. Phillipsburg: P&R, 2011.

Tozer, A. W. *The Root of Righteousness*. 1955. Reprint, Chicago: Moody, 2015.

Vines, Jerry, and James L. Shaddix. *Power in the Pulpit: How to Prepare and Deliver Expository Sermons*. Revised ed. Chicago: Moody, 2017.

———. *Progress in the Pulpit: How to Grow in Your Preaching*. Chicago: Moody, 2017.

Washer, Paul. "How to Reform a Church and Not Be a Coward." Interview. https://www.youtube.com/watch?v=rMeBbeuSYt8&t=1s.

Watson, Thomas. "The Art of Divine Contentment: An Exposition of Philippians 4:11." Sermon, St. Stephen's Walbrook, London, UK, Date unknown. https://ccel.org/ccel/watson/contentment/contentment.xvii.html?highlight=Rule%2018&queryID=1490 2552&resultID=183445#highlight.

Wax, Trevin. *Gospel-Centered Teaching: Showing Christ in All the Scripture*. Nashville: B&H, 2013.

Whitney, Donald S. *Spiritual Disciplines for the Christian Life*. Colorado Springs: NavPress, 1991.

Wilson, Jared C. "Thoughts on the Restoration of Fallen Pastors." *TGC Blogs*. *The Gospel Coalition*, December 7, 2017. https://www.thegospelcoalition.org/blogs/jared-c-wilson/thoughts-restoration-fallen-pastors/.

Witherington III, Ben. *The Acts of the Apostles: A Socio-Rhetorical Commentary*. Grand Rapids: Eerdmans, 1998.

York, Hershael W., and Bert Decker. *Preaching with Bold Assurance*. Nashville: B&H, 2003.

www.ingramcontent.com/pod-product-compliance
Lightning Source LLC
Chambersburg PA
CBHW050827160426
43192CB00010B/1924